Straight from the Hood

Amazing but True Gangster Tales

By Ron Chepesiuk and Scott Wilson

Strategic Media, Inc.

Rock Hill, South Carolina, and Thunder Bay, Canada

13-digit ISBN 978-0-9842333-3-5
10-digit ISBN 0-9842333-3-4

For Magdalena, my wife, my inspiration and love of my life
—Ron Chepesiuk

For Scott Wilson Junior, my son, who I love more than life itself
—Scott Wilson

INTRODUCTION

Many books have written about the black gangster. They have been, for the most part, lengthy tomes focusing on the kingpins of the gangland scene, gangsters with names like Nicky Barnes, Frank Lucas, Lorenzo Fat Cat Nichols and Kenneth Supreme McGiff. Yet there are many stories about the black gangster that have not received much press coverage or have simply been ignored or missed by the media. They indeed reveal a lot about the history of the hood. Straight from Hood is a compilation of some of those fascinating stories

In the following pages, you will find tales feature drug kingpins, entertainers, hit men, street gangs, con men, corrupt cops and reformed gang bangers. Read about the most feared man in the entertainment industry, the love story between Fran, a former heroin addict, and Donnie, a reformed gangster, both of whom have become celebrities; the unlikely alliance between an ambitious Black gangster and a violent—indeed crazy-- white Italian-American mobster; the terrorist plot involving a Chicago street gang, and more.

Did you know old "Scarface" Capone had an impact on the Chicago's African American community? What does Alcatraz have to do with Harlem's most famous godfather? Why is Denzel Washington in this book? Who is a modern day desperado who died by the gun but managed to live on through rap music? How did a stick-up artist from Brooklyn become Hip-Hop's Answer to Lee Harvey Oswald?

Each of the following stories may be amazing, but all of them are true. Straight from the hood. They have been gathered for your reading pleasure. We want to inform, educate and enlighten you. We hope you will be entertained. So read on!

TABLE OF CONTENTS

ONE

Al "Scarface" Capone—Impresario to Chicago's Black Musicians

Al "Scarface" Capone

THE FEDERAL GOVERNMENT closed Storyville down in 1917 during World War I over the objections of New Orleans' city hall, claiming that the district was a threat to national security. In reality, many Americans of the early 20th century were not comfortable with what they heard about Storyville. For them, it was an integrated den of sin, which, as one New Orleans guidebook explained; "held out the allure of sex across color lines, even though segregation legislation was passed in New Orleans in 1894."

With Storyville's closure, New Orleans' jazz musicians had to find work, so many of them joined the flood of black migrants from the south and ended up in Chicago, the Windy City, making the metropolis America's jazz capitol and one of the country's most exciting cities of the 1920s. The nightlife came with gambling, alcohol and prostitution. Gangsters often owned the clubs and nightclubs in the Black Belt, and as Walter Reckless, the author of Vice in Chicago, noted: "They were important links in the chain of beer running operations conducted by different gangs."

Two prominent white gangsters, the notorious Al "Scarface" Capone and his brother, Ralph, were frequent visitors to Southside night spots; in fact, they became two of the most important jazz impresarios in Chicago. In the segregated and often violent world of the early 20th century Chicago, Al Capone became an ardent champion of some of jazz's great black practitioners.

Born on January 17, 1899, to Italian American immigrant parents, Al grew up, along with Ralph and his other siblings, on the mean streets of Brooklyn. Denied a proper education, he grew up a near illiterate gang member who dropped out of school in the sixth grade after he slugged a teacher. By his late teens, Al was, at 5' 10" and 225 pounds, a cocky, beefy, street smart alley-fighter. Tough men could wet their pants in his presence, knowing that he could kill within an eye blink. A few of Capone's brawls involved vicious knife fights, and that is how he earned his nickname: "Scarface."

Al's mentor was Johnny Torrio, one of gangster New York's brightest lights, who worked as a lieutenant for crime boss Paul Kelley in the Five Points Gang. With 1,500 members, the Five Points Gang was the most powerful in New York during the early 20th century.

Around 1915, Torrio moved his operations to Chicago, where his uncle Big Jim Colisimo was the godfather of organized crime. Meanwhile back in the Big Apple, Capone had brutally killed a man in a fight and was laying low from the police. Scarface accepted Torrio's invitation to come to Chicago, and in 1919 Capone headed west with his wife and kid. Al's brother Ralph followed him to Chicago about a year later. The two shared an apartment while they both worked for Torrio in the vice trade.

The Capones arrived in the Windy City at about the time Prohibition became the law of land. Colisimo's extensive vice, gambling and labor racketeering operations made him Chicago's leading gangster. The ambitious Torrio arranged a hit on Uncle Jim and took over his criminal empire. The hitman?—Al Capone. When Torrio and Capone were pulled into police headquarters for questioning about Uncle Jim's murder, a sad faced Scarface told police officers "Mr. Colosimo and me both loved opera. He was a grand guy."

This profitable business arrangement remained in place until January 1925, when some fellow Italian American gangsters shot and nearly killed Torrio. The godfather survived, but he decided he had enough of the gangster life. He retired and moved to Italy with elderly grandmother. At 25 years of age, Al Capone was now head of Chicago's biggest gang.

Prohibition was making the godfather rich and he reveled in the role of the generous godfather spending lavishly on those around him. Capone's flamboyant style captured the imagination of main stream American, and he became a high profile celebrity, just like famous professional athlete and movie stars of the day.

What is not as well known is Scarface's relationship with black Chicago. He bought the Plantation Cafe, a black and tan cabaret located at 338 East 38th Street near Calumet Avenue, which Edward Fox and Al Turner initially owned. The Plantation Café, which featured King Oliver's Dixie Syncopators, had a notorious reputation as a gangster haunt for undesirables. After Scarface took charge, the ultra violent gang wars in Chicago heated up, and in the spring of 1927, the Plantation Café was bombed several times.

Many people in the jazz world of Harlem's Black Belt, depended upon Capone for work and business and he loved it. "To the musicians burning to make names for themselves or simply desperate to work, the Capone brothers, Al and Ralph, were the men to see," writes Capone biographer Laurence Bergreen. "Although the majority of the musicians were black, (Al) Capone, as an equal opportunity employer and corruptor, drew no racial distinctions. Everyone was welcome to join his coalition." All Scarface asked was for ""members' to be loyal consumers for his bootleg booze."

Milt "Judge" Hinton, a famous African American bassist, recalled how Capone approached his uncle, John Thomas, a bootlegger who controlled alcohol sales in his Southside neighborhood. "You buy all the alcohol from me for six dollars a gallon and sell it for $18 dollars," Capone instructed Thomas. "You keep $12 for every gallon of alcohol. I'll handle all the police. You won't have to worry about protection. I'll furnish all the transportation. All you have to do is deliver the alcohol and collect the money. Just don't buy from anybody but me."

It was an offer many people in Chicago, black as well as white, could not refuse, especially when they knew what the consequences could be. Scarface was a tyrant with a mercurial temper who had murdered hundreds, if not thousands, associates and foe alike. An audience with Capone was the last thing one wanted to experience.

But that is what happened one night to the legendary Fats Waller, renowned lyricist, singer and pianist, when some white men kidnapped and hustled him into a waiting limousine. Waller found himself in a lounge in the lilly-white Chicago suburb of Cicero, Capone's stronghold. There waiting for him was your friendly, smiling godfather, who ordered the petrified Waller to sit at the piano and play. Waller began to relax, realizing he was the special entertainment at Al Capone's birthday party.

The bash turned out to be the time of the entertainer's life. Waller performed and partied with Scarface for three days, and then went home, exhausted, his pockets bulging with thousand of dollars. It was the first time Waller had tasted champagne.

While Scarface may have been more racially tolerant than his fellow gangsters, it would be wrong to conclude that he was an early American paragon of civil rights virtue. The white mob in Chicago and other major U.S. cities controlled the jazz scene in the 1920s and '30s as a musical version of a plantation system.

Capone, moreover, had designs on the policy and other gambling rackets thriving in the Black Belt. By the 1920s, an estimated 50 percent of the black population of Chicago played policy, and the game became so big and popular that one found a numbers bank on every corner and in many of the district's markets, barbershops and the backrooms of stores, The policy banks stayed open from 5 a.m. to 1 a.m. and were served by runners who meticulously recorded the gigs on tiny slips of papers.

Capone planned to make his move by first taking over the policy wheel on 35th St. near Indiana Avenue, operated by a man named Roberletto. Sam Ettleson, the powerful senator from the second congressional district, and another senator named Marks learned of the godfather's plans and told Capone to give up the idea. Why they did so is not known, but Capone did tell his men stay out the Southside policy racket. In return, the black gambling establishment agreed to stay out of the bootleg beer business.

Chicago's black criminal underworld had managed to arrange a truce with young Scarface, America's most famous gangster.

TWO

The First Kidnapping of a Wealthy African American

Caspar Holstein

CASPAR HOLSTEIN IS remembered as one of the most colorful and interesting characters in Harlem history. During the 1920s Holstein was not only one of the biggest number kings in the neighborhood but also an important philanthropist who used the huge sums of money he made in the numbers racket for philanthropy. Indeed, Holstein is considered a great benefactor of the famous Harlem Renaissance, the famous movement that nurtured African American writers and artists.

Holstein is also remembered as the first wealthy black man to be kidnapped and held for ransom. On September 21, 1928, at a little after midnight, Holstein left the Turf Club and was chauffeured in his new Lincoln sedan to 225 West 146th Street, the home of his friend Gomez Whitfield. Not finding Whitfield at home, Holstein stepped out of the door of the apartment to cross the sidewalk to his Lincoln where his chauffeur was waiting. Suddenly, an automobile drew up at the curb and several white men with guns jumped out. Holstein later told police that five white men surrounded him, while two white women sat in the car.

The men pretended to be cops. "We want you to come to the headquarters," one of them said to Holstein, as they nudged him into the car. "I have no problem going with you, but why the headquarters?" Holstein asked, as he got the queasy feeling he was being kidnapped.

The response was a vicious hit to his head with the butt of a gun. A couple of the other kidnappers slapped him around. They then blindfolded, gagged, and bound him, as he lost consciousness for a spell. The car screeched to halt in front of a house, and the kidnappers dragged Holstein to the bedroom where they removed his bonds. About $72 in cash and a diamond ring worth $3,000 were taken from him, Holstein later told the police. His hands and feet were then bound securely with wire and cloth and the kidnappers threw him on the bedroom floor. Two of the kidnappers stood guard over him.

After several hours, Holstein was again blindfolded and driven to another house, which he believed to be near the first. He was held there all day Saturday, and then was again brought back to the first house and put in the bedroom. This time he was blindfolded and could see nothing. Why was I kidnapped? The victim wondered anxiously. The kidnappers had not yet asked him for money.

Meanwhile, Holstein's disappearance had caused quite a stir in New York City. The news of the kidnapping stunned white New Yorkers, who were fascinated by the case. They were unaware of wealthy Negroes in Harlem involved in the numbers racket.

In its September 29, 1928 issue, the New York Times reports that Holstein, with "an expert eye for a winning horse," had amassed a fortune through "spectacular plunges on the races." The newspapers also noted that Holstein was alleged to be a numbers banker. Rumors abounded about how the numbers king had lost $30,000 at the Belmont racetrack during the week before the abduction. Maybe he was kidnapped because he owed gamblers money. Or maybe he was robbed for the huge sums of money he was known to carry on him at all times. Others had a different notion. Some were sure that the Italians Mobsters or bootleggers or Chicago racketeers planning to expand their operations into the Big Apple were holding Holstein for money or information.

The Harlem community did not forget their benefactor in his time of need. Several hundred Harlemites, many of whom had been aided by the numbers king's generosity, volunteered to help find him. New York Police Department detectives at the 125th Street Precinct began an investigation, but had few clues.

Holstein's friends, aware of his disappearance, did not report it until Friday for fear police intervention would lead to his killing. Then, on Sunday morning, a man telephoned the Turf

Club and spoke to Charles King, the club's secretary. "Go to the office in a store at 182 Lebanon Avenue in the Bronx," the caller ordered.

The police later identified the office as belonging to 32-year-old Michael Bernstein. Before calling King, Bernstein had gone to a branch office of the American Exchange–Irving Trust

Harlem, 1920s

Company at Southern Boulevard and 167th Street, the Bronx. Bernstein asked the bank if a check drawn by Holstein from an account at a branch of the Chelsea Exchange Bank in the amount of $3,200 would be honored. No, it would not, the teller told Bernstein. Bernstein then telephoned King again and demanded $50,000 in ransom.

Meanwhile, the police followed up on some leads and brought 27-year-old Peter Donahue and 28-year-old Anthony Dagostino in for questioning. While they were being interrogated, Dennis Armstrong, an official of the Monarch Lodge

45, Black Elks, of which Holstein was a prominent member, received a telephone call at his house. The caller claimed to be Holstein.

"The police should get out," the caller warned. "If they continue, all they will get will be my dead body." The police then made two more arrests in the case: Moe "Monkey" Schubert, a waiter, and Rudolph Brown, a black 32-year-old self-described dance hall manager.

On Monday morning at about 2:00 p.m., Holstein walked unannounced into the Turf Club, where many of his admirers and supporters were gathered, dejected and expecting the worst. They embraced the numbers king with joy and he explained what happened. The kidnappers drove Holstein to 140th and Amsterdam Street, where they gave him three dollars for the taxi ride back to his house. Instead, Holstein took a cab to the Turf Club.

"Holstein's appearance was quite unkempt, but he appeared to smile a little brightly for a beaten man without food three days," the Amsterdam News wrote. "He wore a gray suit and overcoat. Bloodstains were on his fancy purple shirt, but none on his striped tie. His shirt was open at the throat."

At this time, Holstein was suing the Amsterdam News for $100,000 for defamation of character because the newspaper had published a story insinuating he might have a relationship to a police case involving the numbers racket. The suit was later dropped. After the celebration at the Turf Club, Holstein went to the police station and told the authorities what he knew.

The five men whom the police picked up for questioning were charged with Holstein's kidnapping. The numbers king never said if he paid a ransom, and many of the details of the kidnapping would remain a mystery. The genie, however, was out of the bottle and all of New York City—including the Mafia—now knew about the Harlem numbers racket and the big money it made. With the harsh glare of publicity on him, Holstein apparently decided the attention of being a prominent numbers banker was not worth it, and gradually withdrew from the game.

The police, however, now were well aware of Holstein's activities and began watching him more closely. Moreover, during the ensuing years, Holstein would have several disagreements with the IRS over his income tax returns.

It took years before the authorities were finally able to get Holstein. On November 21, 1935, police raided his headquarters at the Turf Club and arrested him for operating what the press described as an "insignificant" numbers game. James J. Wilson, Special Assistant District Attorney, said the operation was Holstein's "attempt to make a comeback in the old racket." That could well have been because the man, whose name was once synonymous with the Harlem numbers game, told one of the arresting officers he was "broke."

On January 31, 1936, a court found Holstein guilty. He served less than a year in jail. In the wake of the trial, the New York Times described Holstein as the "deposed head of the Harlem rackets who was credited with having made millions in the racket before Dutch Schultz decided to supersede him."

Holstein claimed that before his arraignment, he was harassed repeatedly by police, arrested several times without cause, and forced to close his Turf Club and spend tens of thousands of dollars employing security guards to protect his life and property.

Two years later, when Holstein was out of prison, police questioned him about the near-fatal shooting of musician Fats

Waller, which happened at his Turf Club. Police reports of the incident support the opinion that Holstein was no longer a big player in the numbers racket.

Holstein's remaining years passed quietly. He was sick the last two years of his life and died on April 19, 1944, at the home of his friends Mr. and Mrs. Alverstone Smothergill. The former numbers king was buried five days later, following funeral services attended by hundreds.

THREE

The Numbers Queen, the Dutchman and Harlem's Battle Royal

Stephanie St. Clair

IN 1912 A remarkable woman named Stephanie St Clair with the nickname of "Queenie" arrived in Harlem, New York from Marseilles, France. Two decades later, a Battle Royal with one of New York City's most powerful white mobsters would make her a legend in Harlem.

The details of St. Clair's life are sketchy, but it is believed she was born in Martinique, a small island in the Caribbean region. She was about 26 years old when she landed in New York City.

Entrepreneurial in spirit, St. Clair soon found economic opportunity. It is not clear how St. Clair did it, but it is believed she accumulated $10,000 by 1922, a sizeable sum of money in those days. What is certain is that Queenie used the money to launch a number operation that made her rich. The numbers racket has long history in the black and Hispanic neighborhoods of the Big Apple, as well as other major American cities. Traditionally the numbers game has been based on lottery policy numbers (12 numbers drawn from a pool of 78), which was determined by a complex drawing requiring a structured organization to figure out the winning numbers.

But during the early 1920s, at the time St. Clair was getting into the racket, the rules of the game had changed considerably. The betting scheme was simplified, and the winning numbers selected became based on the daily closing results of the New York Stock Exchange. The winning total paid at 600 to one, and the beauty of the new system was that, by having the numbers recorded daily in the newspaper, the game could not be fixed.

For a mere 10-cent bet, a numbers player could make $60, a sizeable return in 1920s Harlem, one of the poorest neighborhoods in New York City. The numbers racket became a strong tradition in the neighborhood, and even though it was a nickel-and-dime game, people from all economic backgrounds played. One observer described the game as "the most widespread form of law breaking in Harlem."

Entering the numbers racket at the right time, the charismatic St, Clair thrived in that underworld environment and did quite well for herself. By the late 1920s, she was using 20 controllers and 40 numbers runners to haul in an estimated $350,000 annually, making her one of the richest-- if not the richest-- black woman in America.

Harlem, 1930s

Queenie's personality was as full as her pocketbook, and it was with good reason that Stephanie St. Clair became known as "Queenie." She could be flamboyant, brazen, or generous, and as unpredictable as stormy weather. At 5'8", she was a husky but attractive woman. Old-timers from Harlem would later remember St. Clair as having an imperious presence and as being an aficionado of the finer things of life, which included cloths and the opera.

Given her fiery and fearless nature, Harlemites would also refer to St. Clair as the "Tiger from Marseilles." No doubt, she was the type of person, man or woman, you wanted on your side when the going got tough.

In growing her numbers business, Queenie was soon knee deep in corruption New York style. When a police officer from the NYPD's Sixth Division threatened to arrest her, Queenie scoffed and told him that he had nothing to support the charge. The policeman suggested that they go to the 123rd Street

Station and talk it over with his superior, the lieutenant. She agreed and met the lieutenant, who explained the nitty-gritty of how the streets of Harlem worked.

In 1931, the Seabury Commission began an investigation into the massive corruption in New York City's government. Named after Judge Samuel Seabury, a crusading crime investigator and scion of a prominent New York City family, the investigation lasted two years and probed the relationship between police, politicians and gangsters. Queenie was one of the star witnesses, testifying that she ran a numbers bank from 1923 to 1928 and had ended up paying bribes totaling about $7,100 to members of the police department. It was done, she said, to protect her workers from arrest.

Queenie did not hold back her punches. In her autobiography, Strangers at the Party, Helen Lawrenson explained: "St. Clair accused a district attorney, two judges, and scores of police, bondsmen, and political fixers. She gave names, dates, and the amount paid out in graft."

Her testimony helped get a police lieutenant and 30 other police officers suspended from duty. The brash St. Claire gave a warning to Tammany Hall: "Many more . . . will be in the same predicament if they do not stop framing colored people."

Although St. Clair's high-profile public utterances drew the attention of the white power structure, it appears that the Harlem community largely supported her. After her Seabury Commission testimony, Queenie felt vindicated, but still had to go into hiding, fearing retaliation.

Corruption in Tammany Hall was not the only topic of inquiry for the Seabury Commission. A number of major Harlem numbers bankers were compelled to testify, and under close scrutiny, their revelations cast further light on the lucrative

Harlem numbers racket. Several numbers kings had to reveal their incomes from the racket, and the figures were eye-opening. For instance, by examining the personal bank accounts of one numbers runner, Jose Enrique Miro, the Seabury Commission learned that, in six of his nine accounts, Miro had deposited $1,111,730; in the other three, another $139,826. between January 1, 1925 and December 31, 1931, another numbers king named Wilfred Adolphus Brunder deposited in various accounts $1,753,342.33 of unreported income, according to the Seabury Commission investigation.

Given the money involved, it would just be a matter of time, though, before a powerful white gangster would get smart and move into Harlem to organize the rackets. Any gangster with a little gray matter could discern that Prohibition would soon be over, and they would have to look for new rackets to corner.

The organizing force turned out to be a ruthless gangster with a hair-trigger temper and a one-dollar haircut. Dutch Schultz would make the numbers racket more profitable than it had ever been. But along the way, he would stumble into a war of attrition with another charismatic queenpin named Stephanie St. Clair, who challenged his best-laid plans.

In the wake of the Seabury investigations, Schultz made his move to conquer the Harlem numbers racket, employing the same strategy and ruthless efficiency that he used to muscle into the other rackets he dominated. As individual operators without firepower or real political connections, the black numbers kings were powerless to stop the white interloper. Schultz began picking off the big numbers bankers one by one.

Stephanie St. Clair refused to kowtow to the Dutchman, and she tried to convince the big bankers still outside the Dutchman's noose to band together and fight. "No way," they

Dutch Schultz

said. How could they fight the Mob and City Hall at the same time? They were in cahoots. So Queenie organized the smaller bankers who operated outside of Schultz's influence.

The Dutchmen got impatient with the troublemaker and put out a contract out on her life. Queenie went into hiding. "I'm not afraid of Dutch Schultz or any man living," the policy queen declared. "He'll never touch me." Schultz's men went looking for Queenie; the intense manhunt at one point forced her to hide in a coal cellar, where she lay buried under a pile of coal.

In the end, however, Queenie fought a losing battle. Schultz's fire power and Mob muscle were too much. Her involvement in the numbers racket effectively ended when she went to jail for shooting Sufi Abdul Hamid, her unfaithful husband.

And Dutch Schultz? He became a target of a hit by his fellow mobsters. But before he died and while he lay unconscious in the hospital, the Dutchman received a telegram from Stephanie St. Clair. It read: "Don't be yellow. As you sow, shall you reap."

Stephanie St. Clair eventually faded from history and little is known about the rest of her life. When Queenie died in 1969, the world did not take notice.

FOUR

Bumpy Johnson and the Mother of All Prison Breaks

Bumpy Johnson

WHEN PEOPLE HEAR a supposedly true story about the underdog beating the odds, they cling to it. This makes sense, since America is a country that likes to believe in the impossible. The history of American crime is rife with tales of the underdog beating the odds.

The story of Frank Matthews beating both the Italian mafia and the American legal system by disappearing with millions comes to mind. Though it sounds highly unlikely it did, in fact, happen. Though some believe that the Mob eventually did catch up to the irrepressible Matthews, there is concrete evidence to suggest that he may have gotten away with the biggest disappearing act in history.

Another such story revolves around an escape proof prison and three men who proved it to be quite the opposite. They may have done so with the help of one of the most famous Harlemites in history.

Alcatraz island was once the most famous (or infamous) prison in American history. It is located in the San Francisco Bay, more than a mile away from the mainland. Its location, coupled with its militaristic fortifications, made it seemingly impossible to escape from. Any time served on Alcatraz was hard time indeed. Prisoners dreaded being sent there. Up until its closure in 1963, it housed many of America's most infamous criminals. Al "Scarface" Capone and George "Machine Gun" Kelly are among the more notable inmates to have spent time on "The Rock". Another person that partook of the less than stellar accommodations on the island was Harlem Godfather Ellsworth Raymond "Bumpy" Johnson.

Born in Charleston, South Carolina on Halloween day, 1905, Johnson was something of a child prodigy. By eight years of age, he had skipped two grades. In 1919, his parents sent him to live with his older sister Mabel in Harlem. He would go on to revolutionize its underworld structure. Bumpy boldly took on bootlegger Dutch Schultz and brokered deals with the Italian Mafia that would allow them to peacefully coexist with their African American counterparts. Anyone who hoped to do business in the neighborhood could not do so without his blessing.

By the time of his death in 1968, Johnson had become the prototypical black gangster. He is revered to this day and looked to as an example of how a gangster can carry himself with the semblance of class and duty. He has been the subject of countless books and films that have dramatized his life. To a certain extent, he can be seen as the Harlem equivalent of Al Capone.

In 1954, Johnson began what was to be a nine-year prison term for a narcotics conviction on Alcatraz. Also serving time during this same period were brothers Clarence and John Anglin, Frank Morris, and Allen West. These five men were all doing hard time on "The Rock." Like their fellow prisoners, they likely dreamed about breaking free.

What sets them apart is that they actually tried to make their dreams a reality. By doing so, they hoped to prove that the escape proof jail was just another flawed creation that could be overcome by a truly ingenious mind. All one needed was intelligence, time, patience, and determination.

So on June 11th, 1962, the most daring prison escape in history took place. Morris and the Anglin brothers cut through the walls of their cells. They then made their way to the roof by climbing up the ventilation shaft through one of the utility corridors that lay behind the cells. Once they reached the shores of the island, they paddled their way to freedom in rubber rafts. A search was conducted the next morning by police, but it proved fruitless. The men had effectively vanished. Only Allen West remained behind.

The means through which they executed this amazing feat were cunning indeed. To fool corrections officers performing nightly rounds during lockdown, Morris and the Anglin brothers placed Dummy Heads on their bunks. The heads were made with toilet paper, soap and human hair. An investigation revealed that they were able to use common objects to cut through the walls of their cells over a long period of time. It is believed that the three men climbed fences and constructed a makeshift raft made from raincoats and contact cement, which was launched from the northeastern coast of the island. It is believed that all three men likely perished while paddling through the cold, rough waters of San Francisco Bay. But, to this day, the case remains unsolved.

A popular theory states that "Bumpy" Johnson aided in this historic event. The popular NBC documentary series Unsolved Mysteries claimed that Johnson arranged for a boat to retrieve the three men from San Francisco Bay and dropped them off at Pier 13 in the Hunters Point district. The book Harlem Godfather, penned by Bumpy's widow Mayme Johnson, makes similar claims.

Such a feat could only be pulled off by someone with considerable cunning and resources. Johnson's reputation certainly suggests that he was such a man. He definitely was not short on courage. Skip tracer Frank Ahearn, in an October 2007 article for Yahoo!, claimed that according to his research, Johnson had neither the power nor the money to pull it off.

The Alcatraz escape remains a point of fascination for true crime buffs and historians alike. Even if the men did die in the waters of the San Francisco Bay, the attempt is still noteworthy because it came closest to being successful. As for Bumpy Johnson's involvement, it enhances the image of an already legendary figure in the annals of American crime.

Yet, the June 1962 Alcatraz escape is not Johnson sole claim to fame, or even his most talked about. His legend loomed large even before his arrival to "The Rock." If he did in fact help in the June 1962 escape, he is surely among the smartest and most ingenious criminal masterminds of our time. While his legacy should not necessarily be celebrated, his life serves as a reminder that truly great minds can flourish in any circumstance.

FIVE

The Queen of the DC Underworld

Odessa Madre (r) being escorted from court in the 1950s

IF WASHINGTON, D.C. has a gangster, dead or alive, who can measure up to Chicago's Al Capone or New York City's John Gotti and the legendary gangsters from other major cities, Odessa Madre would be a prime candidate. Her name may not resonate with today's younger gang bangers, but there are still a few old-timers who remember the woman who became known as the Queen of the DC Underworld.

Odessa got that moniker because she dominated DC's criminal underworld for nearly half a century, during which time she was into nearly everything illicit—gambling, prostitution, numbers and graft. In 1990, Miller A. Dixon, a retired DC police department sergeant, who, at the time was 77-years old, said this of the Queen of the DC Underworld: "I had a lot of respect for Odessa. She was the only person I ever met who had just made the decision early on life to be bad. She said: 'to hell with it and went on about her business.'"

Unlike many queen pins, Odessa Madre did not grow up poor. Born the only child of a seamstress and a baker, Odessa inherited property that made her economically better off than most of the black brothers and sisters living in DC during the time. From the sketchy accounts of Odessa's life, it appears that her parents spoiled her rotten. Because of her sewing skill, Odessa's mother dressed up her daughter in fine cloths, while her father let the child empty the till of his business without reprimanding her.

There were a lot of Irish people living in Odessa's neighborhood, and because they allowed the cows to roam the alleys freely, the area became known as Cow Town. The Irish and the African Americans got along, which was a good thing for Odessa later in life because many of the Irish from Cow Town became cops. Odessa was able to cultivate relationships with the Irish cops when she became a notorious underworld queen. Later, Odessa recalled: "Negroes and Irishmen got along real well. They would fight among themselves. If somebody outside of Cow Town came to fight the Irish, the Negroes would chuck bricks at them. We were like a big happy family."

Odessa attended DC's Dunbar High School, an educational institution to which prominent black families from around the country sent their children. While all the students at Dunbar were African American, the shades of pigmentation among the students allowed racism to permeate the school's environment. In 1980, Odessa told the Washington Post. "They'd call me the big black mutha..... There were only three blacks at Dunbar back then—I mean black like me. I had good diction, I knew the gestures but they always made fun of me."

Despite the bad experience at Dunbar, Odessa did well and graduated with honors. Great legitimate opportunities lay ahead for her, but Odessa had other plans. Odessa decided that she would make a lot of money in life and she was not going to be particular in how she did it. She started slowly in her life of crime but would eventually build an empire of numbers banks, whore houses and drinking establishments.

Odessa received an inheritance from the money her family made selling some of its property, and she used it to buy two houses in her old neighborhood. Odessa kept one for herself and used the other one to sell bootleg liquor.

With no real competition, Odessa became a major bootlegger. But not content to rest on her laurels, Odessa quickly expanded into gambling and prostitution. By the mid 1940s, she had a large bookmaking operation and six bawdy houses that employed 20 women. Odessa's entrepreneur ways, both legal and illegal, helped make her a very rich women. The Washington Post reported that at the height of her success she was making $100,000 annually.

Even though Odessa was just starting out as a criminal, it is understandable why bootleggers and other gangsters were willing to do business with her. They thought she would protect them from the law, especially after rumors began circulating that Odessa was in good with the police.

Odessa's headquarters at 2204 14 St. NW became known as Club Madre, a well known night spot that was frequented by many black celebrities. Jazz great Duke Ellington, a DC native, played at Club Madre while boxers Joe Louis and singer Nat King Cole were two of the legendary celebrities who could be seen there.

Club Madre

Madre was known to make theatrical entrances to her club at the appropriate moment when the Who's Who of Black DC was all seated. In a September 28, 1980, Washington Post profile of Odessa, Courtland Malloy wrote: "Odessa would make her grand entrance into the club, mink from ear to ankle. That was a lot of mink, because she weighed about 260 pounds back then. Reserved, in the center of the room, was a table vacant except for a dozen, long-stemmed roses. Odessa would lead an entourage—a trail of about six or seven beautiful 'yella girls,' mostly all for sale, followed by a train of lusty, well heeled E-lite gents."

During World War II, Madre and another noted D.C. gangster named Roger "Whitetop" Simkins started a numbers bank at 1719 1st Street NW, which became known as "The Night Number." Simpkins was a popular gambling king who got his nickname "Whitetop" because his hair had begun turning prematurely white. By 1945 he was a major figure in the DC number racket who reportedly grossing up to $8,000 a day.

Odessa was as good at spending money as she was at making it, and her lavish ways made newspaper headlines. She blew money on expensive clothes and trips, and she was known to buy exotic cars, especially after being released from prison. For instance, in 1968 she bought a Lincoln Continental with a vanity "Madre" license plate. In 1980, it was a Cadillac Seville.

The DC-based Afro American magazine reported how she once entered a store reserved for whites, fully expecting the white store clerk to wait on her. Instead, the store clerk summoned her manager. When Odessa began pulling out rolls of hundred dollar bills, the store clerk fainted. Madre then commanded the store manager to bring her the finest fur coat in the store. He readily complied. In fact, he brought two fur coats. Odessa surveyed the fur coats with a haughty look and proclaimed: "This is nothing but crap." Then with an imperious manner, she returned to her chauffeured limousine.

Odessa was also known to have a generous heart, and she gave away a lot of money to friend and stranger a like. She would befriend somebody in the street and give them money, and she would give the children in her neighborhood money just for being good kids. She would even help to pay for funerals.

Odessa came under intense public scrutiny when the Kefauver Committee asked her to testify before it. But her testimony before the Kefauver Committee revealed that Odessa Madre was a major organized crime figure who ruled the Washington DC police force through payoffs. Unfortunately for Odessa, her high profile appearance meant that she would be constantly in trouble with the law for the rest of her life, although the fact is she had a steady string of arrests dating back to 1935.

The constant legal battles broke Odessa financially, and she was nearly destitute when she got out of jail. It did not help either that her house sitter wrote $15,000 in bad checks while she was locked up. Odessa needed a job badly, so friends helped her get one as a counselor with the United Planning Organization. Now, however, she was a senior citizen, and so she found the job too tiring. The financial stress took its toll and her weight dropped from more than 200 pounds to about 110 pounds.

Still, Odessa managed to wax philosophical about her situation. "Into each life a little rain must fall," she said. "I'm thankful for having made it thus far. The good times are gone but not forgotten."

In February 1990, Odessa Madre, a woman who at one time had been one of the richest people in DC, died penniless at the age of 83. It took eight days for family members to claim her body. Her friends were able to raise $51 for her funeral, but W.H. Bacon of the Bacon Funeral Home stepped forward to ensure she would not be buried in a cheap casket. "She helped a lot of people," Bacon told the press. "She deserved better. She gave me money to bury friends throughout the years."

SIX

One Brave (Black) Man's Stand Against the (White) Mob

Sam Giancana

IN THE 1940S, the Chicago Mob, which was known as the Outfit, was slowly but surely taking over the numbers racket in the Windy City. Eventually, however, one man stood in its way: Teddy Roe, a brash and cocky policy king, whom, like many of his compatriots in the Black Belt, Roe did not like or trust the white Mob. The leader of the white Mob's campaign to take over Chicago's numbers racket was Sam Giancana, a ruthless, nasty gangster who had no respect for black people. Roe regarded Giancana as a snake who had been thrown into the backyard of Chicago's Black Belt to cause harm.

Born on August 26, 1898, in Galliana, Louisiana, the son of a tenant farmer, Louisiana, Teddy Roe moved to Little Rock, Arkansas, as a young boy. It's unclear whether he served in World War I, but by the 1920s, it is certain that he was still in Arkansas working as a bootlegger. In 1923, Roe married and moved to Detroit to work in the auto industry. After losing his job, Roe migrated to Chicago where he settled in the Southside and got a job working in a tailor shop that the Jones brothers owned. In reality, the shop was a front for their Harlem-Bronx policy wheel where Roe worked as a full-time book keeper while pulling numbers on the side at a drawing held at another policy wheel five blocks to the south on South Indiana.

By the early 1950s, Roe was doing so well as a policy king that he could spend $50,000 to decorate his flat at 5239 South Michigan. Teddy Roe had a fondness for the finer things in life. He wore custom made suits, monogrammed silk shirts, alligator shoes, painted ties and wide brimmed hats.

Teddy Roe was a tough guy with a quick temper. He was mouthy, but he could back his rap with his fists, and he never backed down from a fight. Giancana got frustrated when he realized that sweet talk and intimidation, the carrot and the stick, would not work on the brash policy operator. Roe and Giancana butted heads several times. In 1945, for instance, Giancana tested Roe's mettle by trying to shake him down, warning him that Giancana had the full weight of The Outfit behind him. But Roe just laughed at him, vowing never knuckle under to any white gangster.

On one occasion, rumors swirled that Teddy Roe had narrowly escaped a kidnapping. Those in the know said Roe left the Boston Club at 8 p.m., got into his Cadillac and drove south toward Wabash. As he approached 47th St., he noticed a car was following him. He turned east and floored his car's accelerator.

Roe screeched his car to a halt near 47th and Vincennes Avenue, got out and started running. The sedan following him pulled up the curb. Four men jumped out and gave chase, but Roe managed to escape through an alley.

With his fellow policy operators going down one by one as a result of The Outfit onslaught, Roe became the Policy Man in Chicago, and he took over all of the gambling between Roosevelt and Halsted streets. By now, he was making more than $1 million annually, and Chicago's black community loved him for his brave stand against the white mob; it made him a folk hero. Indeed, Roe had no intention of cutting and running. The Outfit tried to work out a deal with him, but he refused, even after his men started showing up dead in alleyways. Shots were that put his wife and kids in danger were fired and his house, bombed.

Giancana tried to sweeten the proposed departure and make an offer Roe could not refuse. The emerging godfather personally met with Roe and offered him $250,000 in cash to quit the policy racket.

"I'd rather die first," Roe told Mooney.

"Well, my friend, you just might," Giancana replied.

Finally, Giancana met with his chief lieutenant Fat Lenny and some of his soldiers in early June 1951 on the Lady Lu, a yacht the gang rented and moored at Burham Harbor. They worked out a simple plan: Follow Roe to determine his schedule and then kidnap him. Once a hefty ransom was paid, kill him.

Shortly after midnight on June 19, 1951, Caifano and three other mobsters began tailing Roe, who was traveling in his Lincoln. They flashed the lights of their sedan, sped up and ordered Roe to pull his car to the side of the road on the crowded South Parkway. The mobsters got out of their car and walked toward Roe's Lincoln. They identified themselves as state attorney police.

"Show me identification," Roe demanded. "How do I know?"

But the would-be kidnappers failed to produce any identification. They jumped Roe and tried to drag him out of the car. Roe was a cautious man and he always carried a gun. He pulled it out and started shooting. Caifano was hit with a bullet to the temple that ripped through his brain and killed him. A bullet hit another of Roe's assailants in the shoulder. The mobsters scrambled back to their car and fled.

When the police arrived, they found Fat Lenny's lifeless body lying on the street looking like a dead beached whale. Roe was reportedly hiding in the bushes. There were no witnesses and the subsequent investigation uncovered no hard evidence about what had really happened.

The police booked Roe for murder and put him extra heavy guard in Cook county jail, following reports that he might be whacked in his cell. To thwart any plot to poison him, Roe's meals were especially prepared outside the jail.

Roe was arrested, but, soon after, the charges were dropped and the legend of Teddy Roe, "The Robin Hood of the Southside" mushroomed. Roe thumped his chest by repeating his vow to the press; "They'll have to kill me to take me."

The killing of Fat Lenny shocked the Mob. It was not use to being challenged and having its murder plots go haywire, let alone to have some South Side black punk take out one of

Black Chicago in the 1950s

their own. On the night of August 4, 1952, two men parked their gray 1950 Chevy behind tow sign boards in a vacant lot across the street from Roe's home at 5239 Michigan Avenue. Fifteen minutes later, the Chevy backed out of its hiding spot and stopped at a red light 53rd and Michigan Avenue. Joseph Turner, a black service station attendant noticed the Chevy and thought the occupants were police men checking for speeders.

He strolled close to Chevy and asked: "Are you guys checking cars?"

"No, no, everything is alright," one of passengers in the car assured him. Turner walked back to the station; in a few minutes, he quit work for the day and went home.

At 10:55 p.m. Roe told his wife, Carrie, he was leaving the house, but did not say where he was going. A few minutes later, five shots rang out. Carrie ran to the window and shouted; "Teddy!" No answer.

She called the police and ran out of the house. To her horror, her husband's bloody body lay sprawled in the street. Five blasts from a 12-gage shotgun had hit Roe in the back, face and jaw. He was packing a revolver, but he did not have a chance to pull it out and defend himself. Roe was pronounced dead at the scene. Ironically, an ambulance took Roe's body to Provident Hospital, the same hospital to which medics took Fat Lenny after Roe shot him.

The hit was front page news in Chicago and a sensation on its Southside. At 53rd and Michigan, young news boys hawked their papers, shouting: "The king is dead!" Police had no clues in the killing, and its investigators could not agree on who killed Roe: The Outfit's hired assassins or independent racketeers, determined to move in on the last lucrative Black controlled policy wheel.

A year later, a police spokesman insisted: "The Theodore Roe investigation is very much alive as far as we're concerned." But the trail was as cold as Chicago in January, and the murder was never solved. It remained one of the estimated 300 unsolved organized crime slayings in Chicago that had stymied police for nearly a half century since the rise of Al Capone.

People knew, though, who had whacked Teddy. It was confirmed in the early 1970s when the FBI caught Giancana on tape, explaining why it had taken so long to rub out Roe. "I'll say this. Nigger or no nigger, that bastard (Roe) went out like a man. He had balls. It was a fuckin' shame to kill him."

SEVEN

Where is Frank Matthews?—The Mystery of a Gangster Legend

Frank Matthews

WHEN WE THINK of famous disappearing acts in gangland, we usually hear speculation about white gangsters like the corrupt Teamsters union president and Mob gofer Jimmy Hoffa and the Irish-American hoodlum from Boston, Whitey Bolger. But the authorities are pretty sure they know what happened to Hoffa (dead, the result of a Mob hit), and Whitey Bolger has been sighted at various times during his ten plus years on the run from the law. So there is no mystery with these two famous gangsters.

But little is heard about brother Frank Matthews, the legendary North Carolina born drug kingpin who dominated the New York City heroin trade in the late 1960s and early '70s. Matthews, who was nicknamed the "Black Caesar," has been missing since July 2, 1973, the day he jumped bail, never to be seen again.

Claims about Matthews' whereabouts abound and are still being reported, and largely because of his capabilities as a criminal entrepreneur, most sources believe he is still alive. "He was an extremely intelligent man who had a strong international drug network and a lot of money," explained Lew Rice, a retired DEA agent who reopened the investigation of Mathews in the late 1990s when he headed the DEA's Philadelphia office. "He's smart enough to hide and maintain a very low profile, and he went out of his way not to draw attention to himself. That combination will bring you a certain degree of loyalty and anonymity."

Pedro Lopez (not his real name) is a former Cuban heroin dealer from New York City who met Matthews during the late 1960s. "I just met him once, but he left an impression on me," Lopez recalled. "He was charismatic, articulate and self-assured. He was certainly the biggest Black gangster of that period, much bigger than Frank Lucas or Nicky Barnes, who have gotten all the attention recently."

So who is the man that draws respect from both a former gangster and a law enforcement official? Born in 1944 in Durham, North Carolina, Pee Wee, as he was known as a youngster, was bright and curious, but he dropped out of school after a year in junior high. He was a natural born leader who even while growing up in the brutally segregated south took no shit from the racist system.

On the street, Pee Wee acted like a budding godfather, a natural-born leader who could get the neighborhood kids to do all kinds of mischief. At age 14, he led a group of eight or nine kids in raids on chicken coops. One of the farmers, a white man, found out that Frank was the ring leader and approached him, bent on teaching the kid a lesson. As the man approached, Frank threw a brick, hitting him in the head. The offense cost him a year in the state reformatory in nearby Raleigh.

Upon his release from prison, Matthews left North Carolina. He worked as a numbers runner in Philadelphia but got busted and only avoided arrest when he agreed to leave the City of Brotherly Love. The next stop was the Big Apple where he again found work in the numbers racket. The money was good but the budding Black Caesar was ambitious. It was the late 1960s and he saw the criminal opportunities opening up in the growing illegal drug trade.

At the time, the white La Cosa Nostra totally dominated the sale and distribution of heroin, and an ambitious young black gangster had to literally kiss the Mob's big pale behind to break in. The drug business on the street while insulating themselves from the actual distribution."

To get his foot in the drug trade, Matthews managed to arrange a meeting with the Mob's powers that be, but they turned him down. Matthews was out in the cold… but not for long. He circumvented the white Mafia by making contact with Rolando Gonzalez, a big-time Cuban drug dealer. Tipped off that the authorities were about to bust him, Gonzalez fled New York City for the safety of Caracas, Venezuela with several million dollars. But before he did, Gonzalez sold Matthews his first kilo of cocaine for $20,000 and promised him more narcotics via his Venezuelan base.

"Rolando became Frank's main source of drugs," confirms Pedro who was a Gonzalez friend and associate. "Matthew got a steady supply at fair prices."

Matthews rise in the drug trade was meteoric. In less than a year, he became New York City's biggest drug dealer, largely because of his intelligence and brilliant business skills. He sold better quality dope than the Italians, thus undercutting them in the narcotics marketplace. Meanwhile, he forged a criminal network in 21 states, consequently controlling the cutting, packaging and sale of heroin in every major U.S. city on the East Coast.

The profits were staggering. In 1971 one drug gang alone was buying as much as five kilos at a time from Matthews' network at prices up to $26,000 a kilo. The gang would then sell about 17,500 bags to as many as 10,000 retail customers for a gross return of about $45,000 daily.

In doing his criminal business, Matthews used the hand as well as the glove. Black Caesar insulated himself from the violent aspects of the narcotics business, but he could be as ruthless as they come when he needed to be.

Matthews, now a drug kingpin, shared the Black Nationalist sentiment of the time. He did not back down from powerful La Cosa Nostra. He warned the Mob: "Touch one of my man and we will drive down Mulberry Street (in New York City) and shoot every wop we see."

In 1971, he organized a meeting in Atlanta of Black and Hispanic gangsters to look for ways to further loosen the white Mafia'a grip on the narcotics trade. By now Matthews was the country's biggest black godfather.

It took a few years but the authorities finally discovered Black Ceasar's remarkable drug trafficking network, and they began to doggedly pursue the investigation. By 1974 Matthews could see the writing on the wall, and as the authorities later learned, he began salting away about $1 million a month in a special bank account in anticipation of the day he would have to flee. That day came in early January 1973 when federal agents arrested Matthews in McCarran International Airport in Las Vegas as he was on his way to attend the Super Bowl Game between the Miami Dolphins and Minnesota Vikings.

Bail was set at $325,000, mere pocket change for a gangster of Matthews' wealth. Law enforcement officials investigating Matthews were livid. "It was crazy," Miller recalled, shaking his head. "I can still see Mathews leaving the court room. I remember him saying: 'We'll see you.' Could you believe that? 'We'll see you.'"

When Matthews jumped bail, the DEA organized a special task force whose sole purpose was to hunt for Matthews, the first time that happened in the federal agency's history. It posted an award of 25,000 for information leading to his capture. The agency was confident it would get its man, but the months stretched into years and still no capture. Sightings of Black Caesar were reported in practically every major American city and as far away as Algeria and Rome, Italy.

Even Nicky Barnes, another drug kingpin, claims to have encountered Mathews in a New York City nightclub, recognizing the voice but not the face. Some of the reports were bizarre. One had Matthews going to a Houston hospital for a heart transplant because it was believed he had a cocaine problem. "We have to check out every lead if we were going to catch him," said William Rawald, a retired DEA agent who investigated Matthews. "But nothing. The trail was cold."

It's now been 36 years since Mathews disappeared. So is Black Caesar one of the few gangsters to get away with it? No one involved in the investigation knows for sure, but they all have an opinion. Most think he is still alive, although they believe he has probably undergone plastic surgery to alter his appearance.

There has been speculation that the Italian American Mafia had Matthews whacked, but as Rawald explained, "Why would the Mafia take risks by killing Matthews? When he disappeared, he left the drug scene and was no longer a threat to it."

In the seventh grade, Matthews wrote an essay in which he outlined his plans to get rich and live in South America. Some DEA agents on the case think Black Caesar may now be living out his childhood fantasy.

This year (2011), he would have turned sixty-seven-years-old, a relatively young age by today's standards. If Matthews is sill alive, time is certainly on his side. "The current generation of narcotics agents would never recognize Matthews because he's not on the law enforcement radar screen," Rice explained. "Thirty-six years is long enough to fade from the headlines."

EIGHT

Crazy Joe and Mr. Untouchable—The Unlikely Gangster Alliance

"Crazy" Joe Gallo

SOMETIME IN THE early to late 1960's, mob soldier Joey Gallo befriended African-American youths from the black-populated enclaves of Brooklyn, New York, realizing that joining forces with African-Americans, rather than fighting them, would be profitable.

The idea of uniting the major African-American and Italian underworld leaders became an obsession with him. It was a point of view later put in to practice by several fellow capos and mob bosses and led to building ties to other criminal organizations.

While in jail, Gallo was an outsider among his fellow incarcerated Italian counterparts and was constantly seen with an entourage of African-Americans. Gallo had no better black friend behind bars than Nicky Barnes. In the mid-1950s, Barnes became a drug pusher, working as a mid-level operator for Dominican traffickers. Caught in a sting in 1959, Barnes was sent off to Greenhaven Prison in Stormville, New York.

Upon his release in 1962, Barnes headed straight back to the drug trade until 1965, when police caught him with $500,000 worth of smack. It was off again to Greenhaven, this time for 25 years. At that point, it seemed that Barnes's life was going to go nowhere except the slammer—that is, until he met Joey Gallo, the gangster who would change his criminal life.

Gallo was a wiry, fair-haired gangster with a short fuse. At age 21, Gallo was arrested for burglary. His behavior at his trial was so weird that the court sent him to a hospital for a mental examination. The conclusion of the psychiatrists who examined him was unanimous: "Joe Gallo is insane." The nickname "Crazy" Joe stuck. Bob Dylan would later compose a song about the growing legend of Crazy Joe Gallo.

Gallo had been convicted on conspiracy and extortion charges in 1961 and was serving 7½ to 14½ years in jail. Gallo and his two brothers, Larry and Albert, ran a gang that was largely responsible for the bloody Mafia war then raging in Brooklyn. What got Crazy Joe put away for a long stretch, though, was his illegal bullying of Local 226, the Automatic Coin and Amusement Machines Employees Union, which represented workers who serviced jukeboxes, pinball, and other coin-operated machines.

Gallo's gang demanded that the union workers pay an initiation fee and monthly dues for the "right" to inspect the machines.

At a congressional hearing, one worker described what happened when he didn't cooperate: "They came out with steel bars and split my skull open... and I was taken to the hospital."

Leroy Nicky Barnes

Gallo was a paradox. He could be a ruthless killer, but often there was lucidity to his madness, and he would astonish his associates with his erudition, often striking up a conversation about Franz Kafka, Honoré de Balzac, Jean Paul Sartre, or some other great writer. The evidence of his punk past to the contrary, Barnes was highly intelligent, a thinker who, when not involved in criminal business, liked to read everything from thick biographies of history's great leaders to dense Constitutional law texts.

Barnes and Gallo hit it off and began engaging in long discussions to whittle their time away. Given Gallo's experience in the Mob, Barnes knew he could learn a lot, especially about how to operate a drug trafficking enterprise. Soon, the monologues drifted toward discussions about organizing the black gangsters in Harlem into a syndicate that could rival the Italian American Mob.

Some sources say Gallo was ahead of his time, meaning that, during an age of rigid segregation, he was not afraid to have blacks join his gangs, much to the chagrin of his racist Mafia cohorts. One police intelligence officer told the press in 1975 that "From what we had been able to determine, he (Gallo) was one hell of a teacher. He schooled a lot of blacks in Attica, Sing Sing, and Greenhaven. He taught them how to move in traditional Mafia territory and they did."

Donald Goddard, the author of Joey, a biography of Joe Gallo, offers a different take. Gallo "didn't like blacks," Goddard writes, and further, he was "a terribly prejudiced guy." Goddard saw Gallo as "a white equivalent of Malcolm X," who was "rising above prejudices... just as Malcolm X rose above his own prejudices."

It is wrong to suggest the Italian American Mobster and the revered black Muslim were brothers under the skin. Still, it is clear that Gallo had to make a move for the sake of his survival; in reality, he had burned all of his bridges to the Italian American Mafia. The bloody war that Gallo had instigated prior to his arrest was actually a rebellion against powerful godfather Joe Profaci. The brash Gallo kidnapped several members of Profaci's family, demanding a bigger share of the profits.

As Mob historians suggest, jail probably saved Joey Gallo's life. He also confessed to sources on the outside that he felt white prisoners at Greenhaven were out to kill him. So, caged and cornered, the only way Gallo could survive was through an alliance with black prisoners.

Barnes liked the idea of an all-black syndicate with him in charge and Mob-wise Joey Gallo playing a seminal role behind the scenes. He knew that crime was an equal opportunity employer in poverty-plagued Harlem. Hundreds of hungry gangsters could be mobilized into a strong force that could be used to overwhelm the Italians. Once the black syndicate controlled New York City, the alliance could easily organize a national syndicate.

Barnes and Gallo struck a deal, and to further the plan, Gallo arranged for his lawyer to work on Barnes's appeal. Barnes's 25-year sentence was overturned on a technicality, and he was released from prison in 1969.

Soon after his release, Barnes called a meeting of Harlem's top gangsters at a bar at 125th Street and Eighth Avenue in Harlem. Barnes used all his charisma and powers of persuasion to convince his fellow Mobsters that it was time they stopped playing a subservient role to their white counterparts. The brothers worked the streets and risked jail, but the Italians hauled in the cash, Barnes reminded his associates.

Coming into the meeting, Barnes had the support of two other Mobsters, Sonny Woods and Hollywood Harold Munger, but he couldn't convince anybody else and his plan was defeated by a vote of 7–3. Organized crime historian William Kleinknecht notes in his book The New Ethnic Mobs that that the meeting was "the closest the nation had ever come to having a true black Mafia."

Undeterred by the vote, Barnes decided he would achieve his ambitions in the drug trade on his own. Many of his workers had stayed on the payroll while he was in prison, and he moved to reactivate his organization. Barnes liked and adopted the Italian American Mafia model in which business is controlled by a ruling council. Thanks to Gallo, he knew the importance of strategic alliances to diminish violence and maximize profits.

Nicky Barnes became known as "Mr. Untouchable" for his uncanny ability to avoid arrest. Barnes was considered so dangerous that, when he went on trial for his crimes in 1978, the made the jury anonymous, the first time that had happened in American history. The popular song, "Bad, Bad Leroy Brown," was supposedly written with Barnes in mind.

"Mr. Untouchable" Barnes was arrested in March 1977, but while on bond, he gave an interview to The New York Times Magazine. The article portrayed Barnes as a clever operator who enjoyed his popularity in Harlem, engaged in a lavish lifestyle and seemed to have made a career out of avoiding arrest and embarrassing law enforcement groups. On the front page of the magazine was the article's bold title: "Mr. Untouchable," with the subtext: "The police say that Nicky Barnes may be Harlem's biggest drug dealer. Now the government will try to prove it."

Uncle Sam reacted like a bull with a red flag waved in its face. The day after the article appeared, Robert Fiske, the lead prosecutor on the Barnes case, received a call from Griffin Bell, the U.S. Attorney General in the Jimmy Carter administration. Bell explained that President Carter said he considered the Barnes case the most important one in the country, and he wanted the government to put all of its resources towards it so we could get the arrogant drug dealer off the streets.

Barnes was convicted and sentenced to life in prison without parole. Behind bars, however, Barnes turned out to be one of the biggest and most productive snitches in U.S. history. For fifteen months, he talked to his former associates, wife and girlfriend as the Feds listened in on wiretaps. And then he went undercover behind prison walls, exposing himself to great harm while gathering information as an informant.

When Barnes "tour of duty" for the Feds finally ended, his information was enough to put most of the associates from his old gang in prison and put more than 50 other people behind bars. Barnes supplied information about a terrorist involved in robberies and prison escapes and testified before congressional hearings and presidential commissions about the inner workings of the narcotics industry and what the government could do about it.

NINE

Frank Lucas—American Gangster or American Fraud?

Frank Lucas

IT IS SURELY one of the most dramatic scenes in gangster film history. The movie is the blockbuster, American Gangster, which hit theaters in November 2007 and is based on what Hollywood claims is a true story. For nearly an hour and half, the audience is wondering how has Frank Lucas done it? How has he smuggled his heroin into the U.S. from Southeast Asia? Then the movie's hero, Richie Roberts, who is based on the real Assistant New Jersey State prosecutor of the same name, who prosecuted Lucas, inspects a military plane carrying the corpse of dead GIs from the Vietnam War that has landed at a military airbase in New Jersey. When, after an intensive search for contraband, Roberts finally opens a casket the shocking truth is revealed. Much to the horror of movie characters and audience alike, our hero uncovers kilos of heroin and exposes what has become known in drug trafficking history as the "Cadaver-Heroin Connection."

It's a great story, one that a suppliant, unblinking media has fueled. Get on the Internet and you will find hundreds of articles that discuss as fact how Lucas used the caskets carrying the corpses of dead GIs—and most likely the corpses themselves-- to poison America with heroin. The reality—there is no evidence that coffins carrying dead GIs were used in such a manner. Many prosecutors and law enforcement officials have their suspicions, but criminals are not convicted on suspicions. The authors research reveals that not one trafficker has ever convicted of trafficking heroin from Southeast Asia via the Cadaver-Heroin Connection.

That is one of many fabrications, falsehoods and outrageous lies that Universal Studios, the maker of the American Gangster movie, together with media outlets like Dateline NBC, Black Entertainment Television and the History Channel, have propagated since the movie's release. The only conclusion to make is that many of Lucas' claims to fame are suspect and American Gangster, the movie, is largely the figment of Hollywood's fertile imagination. Here is the skinny--Lucas is the American Fraud, not the American Gangster.

Let's look at some of the movie's major claims, which Universal hoped would make Lucas a gangster legend:

"Frank Lucas' and Richie Roberts' collaboration led to the conviction of three-fourth's of New York City's Drug

Enforcement Agency. Or at least that's the statement scrolled across the screen. The fact is--not one DEA agent was ever convicted of corruption in the Frank Lucas investigation. Why Universal made that statement is a mystery, but it's irresponsible and the studio should have retracted it. Dominic Amorosa, the federal prosecutor who helped convict Lucas in September 1975, wrote a letter on behalf of Greg Korniloff, a retired DEA agent who was the case agent on the Lucas investigation. In the letter, Amorosa noted that Universal "may have the right to dramatize actual events, this right does not extend to destroying the reputations of honest and courageous public servants by deliberately misrepresenting the facts."

So was Lucas really an informant who just turned in corrupt law enforcement officials and who never took the stand against any real gangsters? The fact is Lucas did take the stand—against a drug trafficker named Leroy Butler. As Amorosa, the federal prosecutor who should know explained; Lucas's cooperation, which was admittedly substantial, was aimed at other narcotics dealers, not law enforcement officers. In an interview with the New York Post, Richie Roberts recalled that Lucas snitched on as many as 150 gangsters.

At the end of American Gangster, Denzel Washington, who plays the Frank Lucas character, made Lucas appear as a victim of the corrupt system, and we were left with the impression that American Gangster should get a medal for his work in cleaning up New York City law enforcement.

Was Richie Roberts really the law enforcement official who almost single handedly brought Frank Lucas down? No way. Lucas was first arrested not by Roberts and the Newark, New Jersey detectives he worked with, but by the DEA and the United States Attorney's Office from the Southern District of

Frank Lucas (r) getting ready for History Channel interview

New York, not Roberts' office, first prosecuted Lucas. Roberts became part of the investigation in New Jersey after the three Newark detectives (Abruzzo, Jones and Spearman) made the case. Richie Roberts, in fact, was a minor figure, in the large scale scheme of the investigation.

Was Frank Lucas really Bumpy Johnson's right hand man? Lucas has made the claim, and given the time that has passed since Bumpy dropped dead of a heart attack in 1968 at age 62, one could guess that few—if any people—were still around at the release of American Gangster to contradict his claims about his association with Bumpy. Guess again. Mayme, Bumpy's widow, was alive and well at age 94 when American Gangster was released. She was mad as hell, too, and devoted her time to debunking the claims of the American Gangster. Mayme co-wrote an autobiography in which she called Frank Lucas a liar and said her late husband never really trusted Lucas.

Lucas claims that Bumpy literally died in his arms, an act that symbolically would make him the successor to Bumpy and

"The Harlem Godfather." The newspapers that carried the news of Bumpy's death in Well's restaurant make no mention of Frank Lucas being present. Interviews with law enforcement officials who worked during Bumpy Johnson's era reveal that they do not remember Frank Lucas, let alone someone with his name serving as Bumpy's right-hand man.

Did Frank Lucas go to Bangkok and establish the Asian heroin connection, which allowed him to deliver to the streets of America the purest heroin ever seen? Actually, this is his how Frank Lucas initially explained it to writer Mark Jacobsen who wrote the 2000 New York magazine profile of him that led to the movie, American Gangster. Lucas had a middleman in Bangkok. He couldn't recall his name, but Superfly gave him the sobriquet of 007. But in the movie, however, it is a character named Nate, ostensibly Lucas' cousin, who takes him to see the Chinese general and initiates the Asian heroin pipeline.

This was false on all accounts. The character Nate is based on the real life Ike Atkinson, a major drug dealer based in Bangkok and co-owner of Jack's American Star Bar. Atkinson, a former U.S. army master sergeant, was able to use the U.S. military to move thousands of pounds of heroin to the U.S. from about 1968 to 1975. Atkinson denies being Lucas' cousin and says it was he who brought Lucas to Bangkok and from whom Superfly got his heroin. Atkinson's claims have been verified in interviews with DEA agents based in Bangkok from the early to the mid 1970s who investigated Atkinson's organization.

Lucas has spun a "007" story. His source of heroin from the Golden Triangle, said Lucas, was a Chinese-Thai. He couldn't recall the source's name but gave him the sobriquet "007. Nonsense, said Atkinson, The source, 007, was really an associate named Luchai Rubiwat and that Lucas got much of his fabled story about the Asian connection by hanging around his bar in Bangkok and listening to American GIs and others in the bar.

So did Lucas become so big that La Cosa Nostra ended up coming him to get their heroin supply? If you believe that, then let us sell you some stock in Bobby Bond's future. It's true that in 1972 the French Connection, which La Cosa Nostra operated, was dismantled, and Asia, as well as Mexico, became more important in the drug trafficking scheme of things. New sources of heroin supply did open up, since La Cosa Nostra no longer had a monopoly. DEA sources have revealed that Lucas was constantly in deep trouble with La Cosa Nostra because he owed two well connected Mafioso $300,000. He avoided ending up in a dumpster only because the two mobsters were arrested and carted off to jail.

Was Lucas the prototype of the new breed of Black gangster: Urbane, articulate, entrepreneurial and, the gangster persona aside, the possessor of a strong moral code stressing loyalty to family and personal responsibility. In reality, Ike Atkinson, Nicky Barnes, Frank Matthews and Robert Stepeney and other gangsters from Lucas' era were more representative of this prototype.

Sources say that Lucas is a near illiterate who had a tough time figuring out how much a stack of hard earned drug money was worth. To catch our drift, compare the manner of Denzel Washington's character in the movie, American Gangster, with the real life Frank Lucas who has appeared on the History Channel, Black Entertainment Television, NBC Dateline and other television shows.

The irony—we would not be discussing Frank Lucas today if that 2000 New York magazine article had not rescued him from obscurity and the welfare rolls. As someone once said: Only in America."

TEN

Bad to the Bone—A Motor City Hit Man's Story

Detroit in the 1970s

IN THE ILLEGAL narcotics trade, there are dealers who move the drugs and then there are the enforcers who do the dirty work of getting rid of the dealer's enemies and competitors. Chester Campbell of Detroit city is one of those enforcers, who are more commonly known as hit men. In fact, Campbell is one of the most notorious hit men ever to come out of the hood.

In 1975 Campbell was arrested for trying to run a cop car off the road in Orchard Lake, Michigan. When the police searched his car, they found notebooks with more than 300 names.

Among them were addresses and phone numbers of political officials, drug dealers and journalists. There were also the names of the victims of unsolved narcotics executions.

It was not the last time that would happen. Twelve years later, in a near carbon copy of the 1975 incident, Campbell was arrested again, as he drove from his house in Detroit's West Side. Police found one shot gun, six handguns (one equipped with a silencer) and the ingredients needed to make a remote-controlled home made bomb. They also found $10,000 in cash and a book containing the names and addresses of what the police said looked like every known major narcotics dealer in Detroit.

"We received information that he is a convicted felon who was in possession of firearms," was all that Kenneth Walton, Special Agent in Charge of the Michigan FBI office, would say about Campbell's arrest.

By the time the authorities were finished searching Campbell's car, they also found personal handwritten records and other documents that appeared to be surveillance reports on various individuals, as well as gasoline, a remote control timing device and blasting caps in the truck. During a search of Campbell's two story house, they also uncovered a shotgun, a Magnum 44 and more revolvers.

It looked to the police as if Campbell was getting ready to launch a one-man war on Detroit. Indeed, Campbell's weaponry made Rambo look like a pacifist. The bust also got Campbell sent back to prison because he already was on parole for a weapons violation.

Campbell's arrest was remarkable, given that he already had served 30 of the previous 40 years contemplating the world from inside a prison cell. You name the crime and Campbell committed it. Try murder, robbery, assault and drug trafficking for starters. "This time I'd hope the (federal) prosecution puts him away for good," said Brooks Peterson, Oakland County (Michigan) prosecutor. "This guy clearly fits the description of a career criminal. He's a threat to society. Of that, I don't have one bit of doubt."

"Incorrigible" "dedicated recidivist" and "heavy-duty criminal" are some of the terms used to describe Chester Campbell, arguably one of history's most dangerous black criminals. One former associate described Campbell thus: "He is a very intelligent person who is ordinarily not given to emotional outbursts. He is cool and conducts himself like a business man and relates to everything in life that way. It is always a matter of business with him."

Despite Campbell's notoriety, not much is known about his life, which is not surprising, given that he operated as a professional hit man. Born about 1930, Campbell went to prison for the first time in 1946 when, as a 15-year old he was convicted of burglary. In 1968 Campbell was released from prison after serving 13 years for the second degree murder of a Detroit man.

Campbell did not show up on law enforcement's radar screen as a hit man until the early 1970s when he was charged with assault with intent to murder a star witness in what became the largest criminal trial in Detroit history, the so-called Pingree Street Conspiracy. The seven-month trial led to the conviction of a group of police officers and civilians for operating a heroin trafficking operation. Campbell had been one of 28 defendants originally indicted in the heroin conspiracy, but the indictment against him was dropped, as was the assault with intent to commit murder charge.

By now, the Detroit police had collected evidence leading them to believe that Campbell was a hit man for drug dealers. When police arrested Campbell in 1975 and put him away, they concluded that the 300 names in his notebooks, which they had confiscated, were possible hit list victims.

Ironically, Brooks Peterson, the Oakland County prosecutor, was on the list. Later, Peterson confided to the press that, during his 17 years as a prosecutor, the only time he ever took extra precautions and security for himself and family was because of Campbell.

Peterson had good reason to worry. In 1975 James Lee Newton, a star defense witness against Campbell, was stabbed to death in a maximum security prison. Guards found Newton's body with his throat slit and Xs carved into his eyelids as a sign of the double cross. Newton had agreed to testify against Campbell because Newton concluded "I figured out they would kill me anyway."

The charges against Campbell were dismissed. Newton's murder was a reminder to the authorities that for them, protecting witnesses when Campbell was involved could be deadly serious.

In 1977, Campbell was finally convicted of being a habitual criminal and sentenced to seven-and-a-half years behind bars. The sentence was added to a 12-year sentence he received early in the year for illegal possession of guns. At the trial, Campbell showed himself to be one cocky mother. When the judge suggested to Campbell that he remove a tooth pick from his mouth, Campbell said: "Why? It doesn't impair my speaking any."

Campbell's life as hit man did come with some risk, evident in April 1985 when he himself was a target of a hit. He was shot while reading a newspaper in an auto repair shop. Three to four bullets hit him in his legs and one grazed his head. From his hospital bedside, Campbell revealed that he had been through an 11-hour operation. A reporter asked for further details. "I have nothing newsworthy to say," the tight-lipped hit man said.

Campbell did not seem to get mad, but one has to wonder, though, if he ever got even.

ELEVEN

Henry Marzette, Jr.—A Crooked Narcotics Cop Who Took Control of the Heroin Trade in the Motor City

Detroit in the 1960s

THE FILM TRAINING Day offered quite an outlandish scenario dramatizing what can happen when a rogue cop gets drunk off his own power. While the plot itself did stretch believability at points, the basic idea is not so far-fetched. Even before the release of the film, the rampant corruption of the Los Angeles Police Department (L.A.P.D) was considered common knowledge to many.

Sadly, that brand of corruption had never really been exclusive or unique to L.A. Every major American city has at least one scandal involving cops that has the makings of good pulp novel. Detroit, Michigan, has one such tale where a rogue narcotics cop not only took bribes and payoffs, but eventually took control of the heroin trade in the Motor City.

The Prohibition era was a financial windfall for crime syndicates large and small. When the government decided to cut off America's supply of liquor, organized criminals were more than happy to oblige. The streets ran red with blood and money poured in hand over fist. Once the failed experiment came to an end, though, the Mafia found itself searching for a new vice to fill its pockets. Heroin was just as good as any. Its appeal seemed to cross racial boundaries. As they had done before, the mob took steps to corner the market so that all buyers would have to come to them. African Americans who wanted in to the drug trade had to get in line like everyone else.

As heroin traffic increased throughout the 1950s, African American gangsters developed their own hierarchy and codes of conduct even though they were supplied by the Italian mob. They also began to pose a formidable threat in the eyes of the law. The overwhelmingly white police department had problems infiltrating their ranks. A black officer could undoubtedly make more headway than a white one (for obvious reasons). Whether they wanted to or not, Detroit's finest would have to diversify its ranks if it planned on winning this particular war.

Henry Marzette Jr., a Korean War veteran, entered the Detroit police academy after completing his tenure with the military. Similar to Leonardo DiCaprio's character in the movie, "The Departed," he was recruited right out of the academy to join the narcotics squad. He was given the necessary tools of the trade, including cars and a wardrobe that would help him look the part. He was assigned to the Livernois and Tireman area, were he amassed more than 100 narcotics arrests.

He appeared to be the as efficient and productive an officer as any department could hope for. Unfortunately, looks can be deceiving.

Marzette began playing both sides of the fence and eventually ended up serving time in prison on corruption charges. While incarcerated, he became an enforcer for the Italian Mafia. It has always been a common practice for mobsters who get locked up to pay black lifers for protection to ensure that stints in prison go comfortably. Marzette did his job well and developed many valuable connections as a result. He was plugged into an even bigger heroin supply. Upon his release from prison, he was no longer beholden to the guidelines of the police department and could now be a full fledged criminal.

In 1960, Marzette targeted a big-time dealer named "Mississippi Red." Marzette ordered three prostitutes to lure the man to hotel room where he waited armed with a shotgun. Thus began his bid for the throne of the Detroit underworld.

As was becoming a common occurrence in any major city where black gangsters and the Italian mob coexisted, Henry Marzette began to grow weary of his Mafia enablers. In 1970, he called a meeting of Detroit's top African American heroin dealers, then known as the "West Side Seven." He planned to organize them into a criminal syndicate that would work independently from the Italian Mob, who were known as the "East Side Twelve." The "East Side Twelve" had plenty of black dealers in its employ, and Marzette wanted to break their control on the heroin trade.

Black gangsters began to resent their place within the structure of the dope trade and sought to climb higher up the food chain. Frank Matthews organized a similar meeting of black and Latino drug dealers in Atlanta Georgia, while the black streets gangs of Chicago began to rebel against Cosa Nostra bosses that held sway over the drug traffic in the Windy City.

Both maneuvers had some measure of success. The writing was on the wall for the Mafia. There days atop the food chain of the American drug trade were numbered. Henry Marzette, Jr. sought to push Detroit's black underworld in a similar direction.

Alas, many of Marzette's contemporaries did not take well to his bid for control and flat out refused the alliance, this lead to a brutal drug war that raged for two years and claimed hundreds of lives. As battles raged in the streets, Marzette fell victim to kidney disease. Perhaps having grown weary of the destruction that his career of choice had wrought, he made one final gesture that would bring an end to all the conflict. He had his top enforcer killed and stuffed into the trunk of a car.

Marzette himself died in a shroud of mystery. To this day, there is scant information available on him. Internet searches will only turn up a handful of leads.

Henry Marzette Jr., once recruited to rid Detroit's streets of dope, instead became a purveyor of narcotics. In fact, he became the chief purveyor. Locking him up failed to neutralize him and only enhanced his rise as a kingpin. As one life ended, another began.

Had Marzette's dream of a unified black mafia in Detroit been realized, one wonders how far he might have gone. One could also wonder what would have become of him had he stayed the straight and narrow as a narcotics officer. Kidney disease cut his reign short, but the legacy of corruption that he represented continues to cripple Detroit, which has become a symbol of all that ails the United States.

TWELVE

From Rapping to Robbing: How Two Groundbreaking Philadelphia Rappers Went From Making Records to Pulling Bank Jobs

Warren Sabir McGlone aka "Steady B"

THROUGHOUT THE 1980S, Hip-Hop culture and rap music were still largely seen as fads. During this time, New York City (the acknowledged birthplace of both the culture and the music) held sway. Rappers from the five boroughs had preference at major labels and soaked up the vast majority of the available media coverage.

It was nearly impossible for any other city or region to break through, but during the late 1980s the city of brotherly love did just that. Their success was short lived as the West Coast was

Christopher Roney aka "Cool C"

also making major headway and would soon supplant the Big Apple as the region with the most popular rappers. This shift in the balance of power left some Philadelphia rappers suffering hard times. Two in particular opted for the "glove and ski mask way" over the microphone.

Warren Sabir McGlone is currently serving a life sentence in Pennsylvania state prison. This is quite a contrast from 24 years ago, when he was helping to put his hometown of Philadelphia on the map as Steady B. While under contract with Jive/RCA Records, Steady B released a total of 5 albums from 1986 to 1991 and was among the first Philadelphia rappers to make noise on a national level. Such a distinction puts him in the same company as the Fresh Prince, better known to audiences the world over as movie star Will Smith. Both Warren and Will started at around the same time, though their careers took wildly different paths.

Along side Warren was Christopher Roney, better known to rap fans of the day as Cool C. Roney was not quite as notable as Steady nor was his artistic output as prolific. He was signed to Atlantic Records and released only two albums, one in 1989 and the other in1990. He was known for taking shots at notable New York rappers of the day such as the Juice Crew. He scored a minor hit with the song Glamorous Life.

Though neither Steady B nor Cool C ever enjoyed gold and platinum sales or crossover success, they were well regarded by knowledgeable rap fans. They did a brand of music that owed much the braggadocio and swagger pioneered by the likes of L.L. Cool J and Run DMC. They dressed in the attire of the day, which included expensive tracksuits and gaudy jewelry. By the end of the 1980s, they had helped to raise Philadelphia's Hip-Hop profile considerably.

By 1986, other cities and regions were making themselves known. Rappers from Los Angeles, Miami and even Atlanta were making headway and even scoring the occasional gold and/or platinum album. By 1989, New York no longer had the playing field to itself. Aside from transcending geographic boundaries, rap's artistic palette was also growing at an exponential rate. This caused the music to divide into subgenres. Among these were politically conscious, afro centric, gangster, Miami Bass and others. The fans had a lot more to choose from, and by 1990 artists like Steady B and Cool C were increasingly seen as antiquated throwback to rap's northeastern roots.

At the dawn of the 1990s, the Hip-Hop landscape had changed immensely. As the Philadelphia's presence within Hip-Hop diminished and West Coast "gangsta rap" began to take center stage, Steady B and Cool C decided to regroup and adapt to the times. In 1991, the two joined another Philly rapper named Ultimate Eaze and formed the group C.E.B, and acronym that stood for "Counting Endless Bank." They signed to Ruffhouse/Columbia records and in 1993 released their debut Countin Endless Bank. The albums title proved somewhat less than prophetic as the album was released to poor reviews and sales. The C.E.B was eventually dropped from Ruffhouse.

No longer able to depend on music as a sole means of support, McGlone and Roney were now in a position they had likely not been in since their pre-record business days. By the mid 1990s, it had become apparent that their run as rap artists was indeed over. While most gangster rappers claim to have left behind a life of crime for the life of a recording artist, Steady B and Cool C were about to do a reverse. Since their recording careers stalled out, they were about to begin a new career as armed robbers.

On January 2, 1996, Steady B, Cool C and another Philly rap artist by the name of Mark Canty attempted to pull off a heist at the PNC bank branch in Philadelphia. Steady B was to be the wheel man. As he waited outside in the parked minivan, events transpired inside the bank that would bring everything to a tragic end. While in commission of the robbery, Cool C shot and killed Philadelphia police officer Lauretha Vaird as she responded to the bank's silent alarm. Vaird had the unfortunate distinction of being the first female officer in Philadelphia's history to be killed in the line of duty. She was survived by her two children.

After the robbery, Steady B was arrested at his apartment. Cool C and Canty had left their pistols at the scene, leaving the authorities with ample evidence. Steady folded under interrogation and gave a full confession. On October 30, 1996, Warren Sabir McGlone aka "Steady B" was convicted of second degree murder and sentenced to life without parole. Christopher Roney was convicted of first degree murder and sentenced to death by lethal injection. On January 10,, 2006, the governor signed his death warrant. His date with the grim reaper was set at March 9 of that year. On February 1, 2006, a Pennsylvania judge gave him a stay of execution until all post conviction litigation has been taken care of.

Rap music (even its crime obsessed variant "gangsta" rap) has long been touted as alternatives to the perils of the streets. Artists with criminal records and the like get into the music business for a rebirth of sorts. Achieving success means leaving the trials and tribulations of criminality in the rear view. Steady B and Cool C experienced the reverse, turning to the gun when rapping no longer paid the bills. While toiling away at a 9-5 is hardly a concession for the glitz and glamour of the rap industry, it goes without question that both of them would rather be working a regular job right now than filling jail cells.

THIRTEEN

The Charles and Griselda Story: New Jack City Meets Scarface

Charles Cosby & Griselda Blanco

IN 1991, CHARLES Cosby was selling ounces of cocaine on the inner-city streets of Oakland, California. Cosby had grown up in Oakland in a little community called Brookfield Village. "In contrary to what it may sound like, it's not a (housing) project," Cosby explained in an interview with the AllHiphop web site. "It was a single family home neighborhood. I was like any other kid growing up in the hood—you know, hanging out.... then the crack cocaine epidemic hit Brookfield in 1983, 1984. So all my friends around me were involved in that and I soon became a part of the fast life as well."

Cosby was bringing in a couple of grand a week and was living the American Dream. "I was living my dream of hood wealth," Cosby explained in an article in the February 2009 issue of Mids magazine. "I had thousands of dollars, a nice car and a few fine bitches. I had the appearance of success. By no stretch of the imagination was I a kingpin. I was merely a face in the crowd."

Then Cosby wrote a fan letter to "Cocaine Godmother" Griselda Blanco who was serving time at a nearby federal prison. "The media painted her as this homicidal maniac – a cocaine queen," Cosby recalled later. "I wrote her a letter of admiration just stating how much I respected her power. She answered back and we became close that way."

Six months later, the Godmother sent an underworld courier to deliver 10 kilos of high grade cocaine to Cosby's residence, and he was a multi millionaire. In 1992 Griselda set him up with 50 more kilos, and Cosby made $3 million in three weeks.

Griselda was incarcerated at the time, but she still generated $50 million per year in the drug trade. Indeed, she was one of the pioneers of the cocaine trade. When she first arrived in New York from Columbia, she had wrestled the cocaine drug trade from five mob families and was soon generating $10 million dollars a week with a network of dealers that numbered 1,500.

Griselda also gave Pablo Escobar his start in the drug trade. Escobar often referred to her as his mentor and when she moved her business to Miami, the godfather was a regular at her Biscayne Bay parties.

Griselda Blanco, the quintessential "queenpin," had several monikers, including "The Godmother," "Black Widow," "The Most Blood Thirsty Female Criminal of Our time" and the "Ma Barker of the Cocaine Cowboys." Griselda Blanco grew up in the slums of Medellin, Colombia, where she was abused as a child and forced to live as a street urchin. She survived as a prostitute before meeting her husband, Carlos Trujillo when she 13 years old. Trujillo would father three of Griselda's children. Blanca was a big fan of The Godfather movie, and she named a fourth son after Michael Corleone, a character in the film played by Al Pacino.

Griselda is, without a doubt, one of the most powerful godmothers in criminal history, as well as one of its most brutal. Her violent crime spree, which may have resulted in 200 deaths in Dade County alone, is believed to have inspired the popular television series Miami Vice.

"She lived to kill and it didn't take much of a reason for her to do it," explained Bob Palombo, a retired DEA agent who for more than a decade played a key role in the investigation of Griselda Blanco. "She would kill those who were close to her and those whom she really didn't know. She left a bloody trail in Miami."

The way the Black Widow killed was chilling. Jorge Ayala, one of Blanco's closest professional assassins, told the authorities in a sworn statement that she wanted Jesus "Chucho" Castro, one of her former enforcers, dead because he had kicked her son in the buttocks. "At first, she was real mad 'cause we missed the father," Ayala said. "But when she heard we had gotten the son by accident, she said she was glad, that they were even."

The Godmother showed no mercy for any of her victims. In another hit, the Black Widow was furious when she learned her hit men had killed a couple who owed her money, but left their three children alive.

Ironically, Blanco picked up the nickname "La Campionsata" (the compassionate one) when she decided against using a machete to kill an arms dealer. The man pleaded with the Godmother to kill him instead with a gun that he had in his car Blanco kindly obliged, saying, "You see, I showed mercy to the man by shooting him."

Cosby ran Blanco's $40 million a year cocaine business while being her lover. Griselda appointed him to run drug hubs in Los Angeles, Seattle, North and South Carolina, Virginia and New York. He became the first black man to ever penetrate her inner-circle. Griselda gifted him with a $20,000 Rolex chain, and she paid the guards at the prison $1500 so she could have sex with Charles on prison grounds.

Still, being Griselda's lover could easily have been dangerous to Cosby's health. Griselda once flew to Medellin to be with a drug trafficker named Alberto Bravo. Eventually Bravo said something that offended Griselda, and she put a gun to his mouth and blew his brains out. The Black Widow ended up murdering two of her four husbands.

Cosby made the mistake of carrying on a relationship with another woman. Griselda was outraged and put out a "warning" hit on Cosby. Shooters shot at Cosby 12 times before he escaped in his sports car. A few days later, he reconciled with Griselda after she reminded him that, due to her, he now grossed $9 million per year.

But when she recruited him to participate in a prison break that involved the kidnapping of JFK Jr., Charles knew he was in over his head. Shortly afterwards, Cosby was contacted by the authorities to give a disposition regarding two murder cases against Griselda Blanco. He cooperated with the authorities, but the case fell apart and no charges were brought against Blanca.

When Cosby returned home, he heard that Griselda had put a $1 million dollar bounty on his head. That contract has yet to be carried out.

Griselda Blanco was released from prison and was deported to Columbia where she lives today. Cosby has parlayed his relationship with Griselda into a lucrative entertainment career. Their true story is depicted in director Billy Corben's documentary, Cocaine Cowboys 2.

So this is the story of a kid from the streets who (literally) got in bed with a Colombian queenpin. The amazing story is truly a case of New Jack City meets Scarface, but it is the truth!

FOURTEEN

The Player and the Panther: How the Pimp of the Year Got Caught in a Black Militant's Crosshairs

Frank Ward, Goldie (Max Julien), Pretty Tony (Dick Anthony Williams), and Tim Ward in a scene from The Mack

THE 1973 BLACK exploitation classic The Mack left a lasting impression on popular culture and gave squares the world over an unprecedented glimpse into the pimp game. Perhaps even more amazing are many of the behind the scenes tales and legends that emanated from the films location shoot in Oakland, California. The most shocking and epic of these is the conflict that arose between a cofounder of the Black Panther Party and one of the most powerful crime bosses in Oakland at the time.

The Mack chronicled the Rise of John Mickens, a newly released ex-con who enters the pimp game and resurrects himself as "Goldie." Goldie's new found wealth puts him in direct conflict with corrupt cops, rival pimps and his black militant brother. The movie was shot on location in the streets of Oakland. At the time, the Oakland underworld was lorded over by the notorious Ward brothers.

The Ward brothers were New Orleans transplants that dealt in the vices of drugs and prostitution. Frank Ward in particular was known for having the largest stable of women in northern California. He tooled around the town in a gold plated Cadillac with customized rims. He sported floor length fur coats and wide brimmed fur hats. His pinky fingers were adorned with multi karat rings. His personal wardrobe was one that would be the envy of any player worth his stripes. His closet was filled with silk shirts, shark skin suits, Italian suits, superfly attire, hundreds of hats, crocodile and alligator loafers and numerous furs.

As was the practice for well known gangsters and hustlers of the day, Frank was known for making quite the scene at high profile events, often upstaging the stars themselves. He attended the Ali vs. Frazier fight in 1971 at Madison Square Garden flanked by his stable of women. Such swagger earned him the respect and admiration of peers all around the country.

It is hardly surprising that when the cast and crew of The Mack decided to set up shop in Oakland they would need Frank's blessing. The film was portraying a lifestyle that he helped to make famous. In an act of brazenness meant to test director Michael Campus' resolve, Frank threw a bag of cocaine down on a table in front of him to see how he would react. Campus then commenced snorting the white powder, hoping that would appease Ward enough to earn his trust.

Ward became involved with the production on a very intimate level, providing financing as well as protection for the cast and crew. He was also something of a technical consultant, too, serving as the basis for Max Julian's portrayal of Goldie. To add an heir of authenticity to the film, he even loaned Julien his car and even appeared in a speaking role.

Frank's association with the production gave the film's crew free range of Oakland. The crew now had access to nightclubs, barbershops, poolhalls, and other hangouts. For a film being made on a meager $200,000 budget, Frank's seal of approval proved to be invaluable. It also benefited Ward in that it gave him a direct line into Hollywood and possibly a more legitimate existence than he had ever known before.

Frank's relationship with the director Michael Campus was not always smooth sailing. When Campus admitted to Frank that the film might not be completed due to lack of funding, Frank made it clear in no uncertain terms that he expected a finished product. Campus found himself under the gun both figuratively and literally.

While this relationship proved fruitful for Ward and the filmmakers, another considerable force that held sway in Oakland took exception. Huey P. Newton and the Black Panther Party for Self-Defense felt the production was encroaching on their turf and made every effort to undermine it. The Black Panther Party was a revolutionary organization founded by Newton and Bobby Seale. They were at the forefront of the Black Power movement. Newton himself had exerted a certain influence on the film, as the character of Goldie's Black Nationalist brother Olinga was loosely based on him.

The Panthers made their disdain for the production known right from the outset. Bobby Seale busted into the hotel room of Producer Harvey Bernhard after Bernhard had refused an invitation to meet with Huey Newton. Bernhard flaunted his association with the Ward brothers, thinking that would stave off Seale. Seale dismissed such boasts with a simple "They ain't shit." Fearing for his life, Bernhard realized that Newton was definitely not one to be trifled with.

Star Max Julien, at the time a friend of Newton's, tried to quell tensions by accompanying Bernhard to a meeting with the Black Panther leader. Bernhard wrote Newton a check for five thousand dollars which subsequently bounced. Such a slight did not go unnoticed. On the first day of shooting, director Michael Campus and his crew were showered with glass bottles by the Black Panthers. According to Campus, Ward took such actions as a personal affront.

Attempts to achieve peace between the warring parties ultimately proved fruitless. Frank Ward and his "Bottom Bitch" were found dead in Frank's Rolls Royce. Frank's bottom girl had supposedly been trying to warn him that there was a price on his head. Ward had been shot in the back of the head, execution style. The Panthers were blamed for Frank's death, and the production was forced to relocate south to the City of Angels. When the film was finally released, it was dedicated to the memory of Frank Ward. In a final show of his considerable power, The Panthers demanded that proceeds from the films premiere go to the Panthers milk fund. The filmmakers conceded.

The rumors regarding Newton and the Panthers involvement in Frank Ward's death were never substantiated. Of course, that did not stop the rumor mill from spinning out of control. The film went on to become the highest grossing Blaxploitation film of its day. It has since emerged as a cult classic that has stood the test of time.

Huey P. Newton was shot and killed on August 22nd 1989 in West Oakland by Black Guerilla family member Tyrone Robinson. Robinson was convicted of the murder and sentenced to 32 years in prison.

Both Frank Ward and Huey P. Newton were charismatic leaders with conflicting views on how to achieve success in this world. They lived out a rivalry that was dramatized in the film itself and died at the hands violent men. However, each left behind a legacy that still influences many.

FIFTEEN

Peace Treaty: How a Meeting Between New York City Street Gangs Inspired a Memorable Moment in a Notorious Cult Film and Set the Stage For Hip-Hop to Emerge

Members of The Ghetto Brothers

WALTER HILL'S 1979 cult classic The Warriors lives in infamy for many reasons, not the least of which are the acts of violence that became associated with the film in the wake of its release. This resulted in advertisements for the film being pulled from circulation by its distributor Paramount Pictures, which had an indelible impact on its box office prospects.

In keeping with the spirit of macho defiance and rebellion that permeated the film, it not only turned a profit but went on to become one of the most popular films of its kind. Though not widely regarded for its realism or accuracy, a major set piece in the film was indeed inspired by real life events. The events in question had a huge impact on the gang culture that proliferated in New York City in the 1970s and helped to set the stage for wholly different culture that would take the world by storm.

In the 1970s, economic and social conditions converged to turn the South Bronx into a virtual war zone. The area became a breeding ground for a number of societal ills, not the least of which was the proliferation of street gangs. Street organizations with colorful names such as the Savage Skulls, The Black Spades and the Ghetto Brothers carved out territory throughout the borough and defended it zealously. Though this was a time long before crack sales allowed street gangs to equip themselves with sub machine guns and the like, conflicts between warring parties were brutal indeed and sometimes resulted in murder.

The Ghetto Brothers was founded by Benjamin Melendez after his family relocated to the Crotona Park Area in the late 1960s. The Ghetto Brothers were among the more progressive organizations of the time in that they showed a sense of political awareness and activism. They had ties to the Puerto Rican Socialist Party and were even involved in music. The Ghetto Brothers served a dual function as both the name of the gang and Benjamin's Latin Rock Band which consisted of himself and his three brothers.

The Ghetto brothers were also innovative in terms of their vision. They made strides toward uniting the people of the Bronx and quelling disputes. Benjamin went so far as to abolish the title of "Warlord" within his own clique and instead instituted the position of Peace Counselor. He bestowed this honor upon Cornell "Black Benjie" Benjamin, a black Puerto Rican who overcame drug addiction. "Black Benjie" became instrumental in the Ghetto Brothers efforts towards peace, even as the violent confrontations escalated. Eventually, Benjie would be swallowed whole by the maelstrom.

Benjamin was killed while trying to stop a conflict between multiple gangs. The Seven Immortals, the Black Spades and the Mongols were on the way to a rumble with the Savage Skulls. Benjie tried to steer them toward a more diplomatic solution, but his pleas were met with violent resistance. One of the seven immortals produced a pipe, the other a machete. After ordering his fellow ghetto brothers to run, Benjie's head was bashed in with a pipe. After collapsing to the ground, he was beaten mercilessly. He later died at an area hospital.

This prompted the Ghetto brothers to organize a peaceful meeting of all warring gangs at the Boys club on Hoe Avenue in the Bronx on December 7, 1971. Benjie Melendez opted for this instead of violent reaction. His decision was initially met with opposition, but he held his stance. In attendance were the most prominent area gangs of the day. The meeting took place in the Gym, where gang leaders hashed out there differences. Among those in attendance was 14-year old Black Spades "warlord" Afrika Bambaataa, better known to the masses as a pioneering force in Hip-Hop culture and the founder of the Universal Zulu Nation.

The meeting proved successful for the most part, with all of the leaders having signed a truce. Still, the proceedings maintained a revolutionary mindset as the police were asked to leave before deliberations would begin. A member of the Turbans gang was given a rifle and ordered to take a Sentry position on a rooftop across the street from the Boys Club to ensure that gang members would respect the peaceful spirit of the meeting.

As the 1970s progressed, the culture of gangbanging subsided. In the wake of the truce, The Ghetto Brothers continued to invite gang members from warring neighborhoods to their block parties in the name of peace, as had been their custom even in the days before the truce. After establishing the Black Spades as the biggest and most prominent gang in the city, Afrika BamBaataa become more politically minded and began hosting the block parties that would become the basis for Hip-Hop culture.

He also became a recording artist. With his group the Soulsonic Force, he released the trendsetting song "Planet Rock" through Tommy Boy Records. The influence of the song can still be felt in a variety of musical genres to this day. Hip-Hop culture has gone on to become a worldwide phenomenon grossing billions and influencing all aspects of popular culture.

As for the Hoe Avenue Meetings affect on the film The Warriors? One only has to look at the story of the film. It focused on a gang from Coney Island that attends a meeting in the Bronx organized by Sirus, leader of the most powerful gang in the city. Sirus plans to unite all of the gangs into one super gang that would control the city. When Sirus is gunned down while addressing the massive crowd of gang members, the Warriors are falsely accused of his murder. They then have to "bop" there way back to Coney Island.

The scene showing the gathering of various gangs is easily among the most memorable in the film, as is Sirus' constant use of the phrase "Can you dig it" to rile up the crowd. The line between fantasy and reality is obvious when one observes that the Hoe Avenue meeting ended in success where as its cinematic counterpart ended in tragedy. Still, it is obvious that the sequence depicting the meeting as well as the film poster was indeed informed by what transpired on Hoe Avenue.

It is quite amazing how something so small that seemingly only affects the people directly involved can have a ripple effect that changes the world as we know it. The living conditions of the South Bronx produced the gangs that roamed its streets. The violence that transpired between them lead to the necessity of the Hoe Avenue peace meeting.

By simply coming together in search of a peaceful solution to a violent problem, The Ghetto Brothers and all other parties involved unintentionally influenced both Hollywood and the landscape of American music. Never underestimate the power of the few, and never disregard the propensity of the disenfranchised to solve there own problems.

SIXTEEN

Wiseguy by Association: How a Bluesman From the South Bronx Aided Mobsters In One of The Biggest Cash Heists in American History

Parnell Steven "Stacks" Edwards

ON DECEMBER 11, 1978, a crew assembled by Jimmy "The Gent" Burke pulled of what was then the biggest cash robbery in American History: the Lufthansa Heist. The heist was immortalized in the annals of modern American crime lore when Martin Scorcese chronicled its bloody aftermath in his modern crime masterpiece, Goodfellas. Parnell Steven "Stacks" Edwards is not so much remembered for the role that he played in the heist, but rather for how he neglected to carry out the responsibilities of that role.

Born in the South Bronx, Edwards was a struggling blues musician who dabbled in petty crime. He headed up a band called Grand Central Station and performed occasionally at a saloon named Robert's Lounge in Queens, which the Lucchese crime family owned. He was a house regular at Henry Hill's bar, The Suite. Though Edwards performed as a musician, he supplemented his income by fencing stolen goods in Harlem. Stints in prison gave him a well muscled physique. He was known to claim that he had worked as a bodyguard for Muhammad Ali, and he was also believed to have been a low level drug courier for Leroy "Nicky" Barnes. Throughout the 1970s, Barnes was Harlem's reigning heroin kingpin and perhaps the most widely recognized black gangster in all of New York City.

Such a resume would suggest someone who was headed for an infamous life of crime. Edwards, however, stayed relatively below the radar and lived an existence that differed little from that of the average petty crook.

In 1967, Edwards became an associate of the Vario Crew by way of a close friendship with Lucchese family associate Thomas Anthony "Two-Gun Tommy" DeSimone. The Vario Crew was run by Paul Vario, a made man in the Lucchese crime family. The Luccheses are one of five Cosa Nostra families that rule organized crime in New York City. The Vario crew itself was a mixture of "made" members and associates, including Burke, DiSimone and Hill.

Edwards became a driver and assistant to Vario crew members. He also began a professional relationship with DeSimone and Hill. Their schemes included car theft and credit card fraud, the latter of which Edwards proved to be particularly adept.

Edwards was known as an expert at "under the limit" credit card fraud. Each day, he would make 45 dollar purchases on cards that had 50 dollar expenditure limits. The purchases consisted mainly of household appliances, electronics and other items. He purchased enough merchandise to fill a panel truck to capacity. He made frequent use of valuable contacts, which included a girlfriend who was employed by Mastercharge. He was also a hard core drug addict, having developed a habit that included heroine and cocaine.

His extracurricular activities did not diminish his value to his mob associates. They cut him in on their biggest score yet when bookmaker Martin "Marty" Krugman shared a juicy piece of info with Hill: large sums of cash were being held overnight in a safe at the Lufthansa terminal at JFK airport in New York. Hill immediately shared this info with Burke and the two realized that a fairly small crew with two vehicles could steal the funds from the safe with relatively little problem. Burke then set about organizing and planning the heist. He assembled a crew that included his own son Frank James Burke, Joe Manri, Robert McMahon, Louis Cafora, DeSimone, Paolo LiCastri, Angelo Sepe and, of course, Edwards himself.

The group used a black Ford Econoline van to transport the significant cash haul. The robbery itself took a little over an hour to complete. No one was killed; however, two agents were violently assaulted and detained.

The heist was pulled off successfully. Edwards was responsible for delivering the panel truck used in the heist to a New Jersey junkyard where it would be disposed of, thus eliminating a major link between the Vario crew and the heist. But Edwards felt a sense of elation after the heist and shirked his responsibilities. He crashed his girlfriend's apartment and indulged himself in a marijuana and cocaine binge before falling asleep.

The Van that Edwards had left in a No Parking zone was discovered by authorities. It was promptly linked to the robbery after police were able to procure finger and shoe prints that identified Edwards as the driver. Though Edwards was able to slip away from his girlfriend's apartment undetected, the damage had been done. The F.B.I had immediately taken steps to investigate and build a case against the Burke and his crew. Determined not to be caught, Burke began a bloody campaign, eliminating any and all links between him and the heist. Logically, "Stacks" would become the first casualty, for his transgression proved to be the most costly.

On December 18, 1978, seven days before Christmas, Tommy DeSimone and Angelo Sepe paid Edwards a visit at his apartment. Shortly after entering, DeSimone shot Edwards dead. DeSimone was believed to have been quite conflicted about carrying out the hit. He had grown quite fond of Stacks; however, his desire to become a made man in the Lucchese family overpowered any loyalty he felt to Edwards.

Joseph Dipalermo suggested that he could achieve membership by handling the Edwards job. In typical mobster fashion, both DeSimone paid respects to Edward's immediate family, despite having killed him. That his friendship with DeSimone would end so bloodily likely never occurred to Edwards even after his big screw up.

Edwards death was reenacted in Goodfellas, where he was portrayed by a then little known character actor by the name of Samuel L. Jackson. Jackson's was hardly a ringer for the real "Stacks," and his lanky build was a far cry from Parnell's jailhouse physique. His character was more or less an afterthought in the otherwise amazing film. He appeared to have little to no relationship with Tommy Devito (a character based on DeSimone and portrayed by Joe Pesci), who showed no remorse for the hit.

In reality, Edwards had a more intimate relationship with members of the Vario crew, thus rendering him more than just a footnote in the recent misadventures of the Mafia.

In a sense, he came closer to being "made" than any other black man in history. That was no small feat for a bluesman from what was then the most desolate part of New York City.

SEVENTEEN

Kingpin of the Caribbean: How a Native of St. Thomas Helped Keep America Awash in Colombian Cocaine

Jimmy "The Juice" Springette, Most Wanted

IN COCAINE COWBOYS 2, Charles Cosby spoke of how black gangsters were traditionally locked out of the ranks of other ethnic mafias. Reputed assassin Jorge "Rivi" Ayala confirmed such sentiments by voicing his own disdain for black Americans. This made Cosby's position in Griselda Blanco's cocaine empire rather remarkable. Surprisingly enough, he was not the only black gangster in history to work so closely with Colombian cocaine cartels. Another gangster of West Indian descent would make a similar ascension within their ranks. In fact, he attained a level of power and acceptance that arguably surpassed that of even Charles Cosby himself.

Born on August 18, 1960, in St. Thomas, Virgin Islands, Jimmy "The Juice" Springette grew up to lord over a criminal empire of staggering breadth and reach. In 1991, he started an organization called "The Island Boys," which established a cocaine pipeline from the Caribbean to the United States and beyond. While Miami's era of the cocaine cowboy had come to an end, Springette showed that its spirit lived on in other parts of the world.

Working with the Colombians gave "The Island Boys" a nearly limitless supply of powder with which to flood the world market. Every two weeks, the Island Boys imported 1000 kilos of cocaine into the United States and the Virgin Islands. The merchandise was delivered via airdrop into the Caribbean from Springette's Venezuela ranch. It arrived in 420 kilogram bales. Once recovered, the bales were broken down into smaller quantities and prepared for transportation to various cities in the U.S including New York, Baltimore and Atlanta.

Springette was truly an international presence, as he operated on three different continents. Though Springette did considerable business in the U.S., he was also stationed in Colombia, Venezuela, Panama, England, France and islands in the Caribbean. He also headed up an international money laundering operation that cleaned $100 million a year. His clientele included mob bosses and organized crime figures from all over the globe. This level of unprecedented success prompted the Colombian mafia to welcome Springette into its ranks officially, thus making him the first black man ever to be "made" by the Colombian mob. He became a soldier for one of the most powerful Colombian cartels.

Such infamy helped Springette make both the U.S. Customs top 15 list and the F.B.I's top ten list. He was the 471st person to make the latter, which likely qualified him as one of the most wanted men in world history.

The Island Boys are responsible for the shooting death of one police officer and the beating death of another. In a move right out of a Hollywood blockbuster, Springette and a group of mob soldiers hijacked a prison bus so they could free two of his Island Boys compatriots who had been arrested. Springette purchased a cargo freighter for $300,000, which was later seized while transporting 6,000 kilos of cocaine.

As shown by the prison bus hijacking, Springette demonstrated a fearlessness and blatant disregard of authority that would give even the most vicious American drug gangs pause. He defended his business zealously, going to great lengths to ensure that his precious cargo of Colombian cocaine would never fall into the hands of police and government officials.

In 1996, Springette and his men fired upon police officers who stopped a van transporting two tons of cocaine in the Virgin Islands. Two officers were wounded during the firefight. In October 1998 he was charged in the Southern District of Georgia with a laundry list of serious crimes, including conspiracy to import cocaine hydrochloride and cocaine base, conspiracy to distribute cocaine and conspiracy to launder monetary instruments. At this point, Springette had been using the city of Augusta, Georgia, as his base of operations in the United States since 1991. He had been enticed to the area by three dealers, two of which were gunned down after they began doing business. One was left paralyzed, the other killed.

Springette was arrested in Medellin, Colombia, on January 30,,1999. He proved himself to be the criminal heir apparent to Harry Houdini when he escaped from La Picota maximum security prison Bogotá, Colombia, on March 1,, 2000. But his talents as an escape artist failed him when he was arrested again on November 5, 2002, at a shopping mall in Venezuela. On September 19, 2003, he pleaded guilty to cocaine smuggling and faced more than ten years in prison on the conspiracy charges alone. He still has yet to be sentenced.

In September 2007 he testified in a St. Thomas Court against six men who helped operate a wing of his drug operation. Like so many other maverick success stories based in the world of cocaine smuggling, the legacy of Jimmy "The Juice" ended not in a blaze of glory or in nose deep in the spoils of war, but in courtrooms and in prisons. It is a rather anticlimactic end to such an extraordinary life, but one that any desperado of Springettes nature would have to see as a likely outcome. Perhaps for him, the positives outweighed the risks. That he managed such a substantial run given the quantities of cocaine he dealt in and the seriousness of his crimes, is remarkable.

If there is one thing that the exploits of Jimmy "The Juice" Springette shows, it is that meager beginnings are no match for brazenness and raw ambition in the drug game. Nothing is off limits. If one shows himself to be a hard worker and good earner, even the most exclusive of organizations will eventually open up their doors and their books to you. Though membership in ethnic mobs and drug cartels is hardly an honorable aspiration, Jimmy "The Juice" showed a dedication and perseverance that transcended racial and international boundaries. If the often repeated phrase "game recognizes game" holds any weight, one would think that Charles Cosby, himself, would have to acknowledge the legacy of James Springette.

EIGHTEEN

America's Home Grown Terrorists: The Strange Case of Libya, Khadafy and a Chicago Street Gang

Jeff Fort

IN 1986, NEARLY fifteen years before 9-11 and the terrorist atrocities at the World Trade Center in New York City, the El Rukns, a street gang from Chicago, threatened to declare War on Uncle Sam in the service of a terrorist state. Jeff Fort, the leader of the El Rukns (formerly known as the Blackstone Rangers and Black P. Stone Nation) founded the gang in the mid 1960s in Chicago's Woodlawn neighborhood.

The charismatic Fort showed remarkable leadership and organizational abilities in absorbing rival street gangs and by the late 1970s, he headed Chicago's most powerful gang. Fort tried to portray himself as a community leader, and in 1980 he had announced his conversion to Islam. But law enforcement believed him to be a drug dealer, extortionist and ruthless gangbanger.

Beginning in 1972, law enforcement was successful in putting Fort behind bars. Finally, in 1983 he was sentenced to 13 years in prison on drug trafficking charges. The authorities sent the gang leader as far away as possible from Chicago: The Federal Correctional Institution at Bastrup, Texas. Fort, however, continued to direct his gang through the telephone calls he made from prison.

In designing a code for his calls, Fort thought he was clever, but with the help of an informant from the El Rukns, the authorities broke the code and began monitoring his instructions to the gang back in Chicago. Soon it was discovered that Fort and the El Rukns were conspiring to commit hostile acts against the U.S. on behalf of a foreign government.

The plot began in early 1986, when Fort discovered that Louis Farrakhan, the leader of the Nation of Islam, had received $5 million from Libyan leader Colonel Moammar Khadafy, who had ruled Libya since 1969. In the 1970s and '80s, Khadafy supported revolutionary movements, mostly Muslim, throughout the world, and he hated Uncle Sam.

The way Fort looked at it, Farrakhan had done nothing to justify the $5 million. In conversations, Fort used the code word "Pecan" to refer to Farrakhan. "We know Pecan wasn't a live soldier from the jump… he's a good mouthpiece, but he's not a live soldier," Fort told his gang in a scathing critique. In other words, Farrakhan was just talk. Fort saw an opportunity to obtain money from Khadafy by showing him that he was willing to carry out attacks on the U.S. for the Libyan leader.

Moammar Khadafi

Fort sent a delegation to Libya to see about getting some money. The delegation included Leon McAnderson, Reico Crenshaw and Charles Knox, who owned an unaccredited law school in Chicago and whom the authorities eventually learned had visited Fort at Bastrup under false pretenses. The trio would later claim that they had traveled to Libya to attend a peace conference, but the U.S. government charged that they met with some of Khadafy's top generals to discuss a deal. In return for perhaps a million dollars a year, the El Rukns would do all it could to help the Libyans attack the U.S.

Fort knew that there was no free lunch with the Libyans, and that his gang would have to earn its money. As the Feds listened in, Fort described in coded language the various things the gang could do to impress the Libyans to show that the gang was serious. We can damage a government building, plant bombs and blow up an airplane, Fort mused. He told his generals that the Libyans should be aware of "what crops we wanted to plant and how long it will take to grow them and how to cultivate the soil.... and let it manifest." The authorities interpreted that comment as code for "the gang needed training on how to make and use explosives."

On April 4, 1986, McAnderson and Crenshaw informed Fort that Charles Knox had discussed with a Libyan general the potential killing a Milwaukee alderman who had spoken out against Khadafy. That would show our loyalty to the Colonel,

Crenshaw told Fort. The leader agreed, stating that after the killing was done, the El Rukns would be like brothers with the Libyans.

But before the gang would do that, Fort needed to know something. He told his generals to verify that the idea to kill the alderman really came from the Libyan general. The El Rukns would only carry out the hit if the request came from the Libyan general, Fort said. According to one government brief related to the case: "The only concern that Fort expressed about the killing (of the alderman), or "canvass' in El Rukn code, was his insistence that they first learn the identity of the Libyan general who requested the murder so the defendants (the El Rukns) would be sure to get proper credit for killing the alderman. Once that was taken care of, the murder itself was no problem, according to Fort.

Toward the end of April 1986, however, Fort began to express doubts that the gang would get some of the money for Libya anytime soon.

Yet, Fort had not totally given up on the Libyans, although he believed they still needed convincing that the El Rukns were serious and would give them their money's worth. In the spring and early summer of 1986, Fort thought of a scheme to impress the Libyans. The gang would buy a rocket, and then use it on one of Libya's enemies.

The FBI saw an opportunity and arranged a sting operation whereby they would sell the El Rukns a rocket. At the time, undercover FBI agent Willie Hurlon was cultivating a relationship with Alan Knox, an El Rukn general. Sam Buford, a drug dealer who was cooperating with Hurlon's investigation, knew the El Rukns and introduced Hurlon to Knox. Now in direct contact with the gang, Hurlon told Knox that he had friend who worked at an army base from which he stole a lot of property.

"Do you know any one interested in buying some off the property?" Huron asked Knox.

"Sure do," Knox said. "I'm interested in buying rocket launchers, bullet proof vests, grenade launchers and infrared field glasses." He described the type of rocket launcher he wanted as the kind used in a recent Clint Eastwood Dirty Harry movie (The Enforcer).

It was a LAW rocket launcher, a powerful weapon that in the hands of a terrorist can do a lot of damage. The LAW rocket's warhead contains a high powered explosive, which after exploding, sets off a blast capable of penetrating armor ten to twelve inches thick. The LAW rocket is designed to destroy an armored tank or penetrate concrete bunker type fortifications.

Hurlon played it cool and told Knox he would check with his friend. Through June and July, Knox bugged Hurlon about the weapons before undercover agent finally relented. Hurlon's friend was ready to deal. Knox wanted five rocket launchers and ten bulletproof vests. The number of bulletproof vests was okay, Hurlon said, but his friend would sell Knox just two LAW rocket launchers.

The deal was in the works, but Fort was nervous. Be careful, he told his generals. Hurlon may be an undercover agent. Melvyn Mayes and Alan Knox (not related to Charles), the El Rukn generals who would make the missile deal, assured Fort that Hurlon was not an undercover agent. Satisfied, Fort gave the green light.

On July 31, 1986, Mayes and Knox went to a Holiday Inn in the southern Chicago suburb of Lansing to buy the first rocket for $1850. Fort was still cautious and he ordered his two generals not be present when money changed hands. Further, they should not bring the rocket directly back to Chicago. Instead, he ordered Sam Buford to make payment, and Roosevelt Hawkins, a low ranking El Rukn, to bring the rocket back to Chicago.

The purchase made Fort drunk with power. "Nobody will be able to stand up to the El Rukns." he told his gang. "We have secured our place in history."

The LAW rocket was a powerful weapon, but its impressive features were academic. The one the El Rukns purchased was equipped with an electronic beeper, not explosives.

It was time for the authorities to move in. For five days since the rocket's purchase, the Feds had followed the rocket via the electronic monitoring device. On August 5, 1986, at 6 a.m., five days after the sale of the rocket, they raided the home of one of Fort's men and found the rocket stashed in a hollowed out stairwell. Fort and five other El Rukns were charged with conspiracy to wage a terrorist campaign against the U.S. in exchange for $2.5 million from Libyan leader Moammar Khadafy.

Today, Jeff Fort is spending the rest of his life in Florence Maximum Security Prison in Colorado, the country's toughest prison, where is under lockdown 23 hours a day.

NINETEEN

The Preacher Man—The Gangster Serial Killer

Clarence Heatley

IN THE 1980S, a vicious killer with the chilling moniker of "the Black Hand of Death," made his presence felt on the Harlem gangster scene. The Black Hand of Death's given name was Clarence Heatley, and he was also known as "the Preacher" for his formidable oratorical skills. The gang he organized in 1983—at the age ripe old age of 30—was known as the Preacher Crew, and it terrorized Harlem for more than a decade.

Most Harlem crack dealers respected each other's turf. After all, there was plenty of money to be made. Preacher, on the other hand, considered all of Harlem his territory. He made a lot of money, not by dealing crack but by extorting other crack dealers. The Preacher would walk up to a drug dealer and take is car or even force him to cough up all of the money he had on him. If the dealer resisted, Preacher killed or kidnapped him and brought him to the basement of his apartment building at 2075 Grand Concourse in the Bronx, which served as the Preacher's headquarters.

"Small Paul" Singleton was one of the drug dealers from whom the Preacher wanted to extort money. Preacher allegedly had Singleton kidnapped and brought to the basement, where he sodomized him in front of one of Singleton's partners to show the partner he meant business. Preacher then had Singleton murdered. As he did after other murders, Preacher had his men clean his execution chamber with boric acid and ammonia to destroy any evidence.

Preacher operated a kidnapping business in Harlem with ruthless efficiency. Dealers were reportedly paying Preacher $20,000 to $30,000 to be left alone. Authorities believe that the crew's kidnapping business was hauling in $1 million annually. The Preacher Crew also served as an assassination squad for other Harlem gangsters. The crew picked up murder contracts in the drug trade for a standard fee of $5,000 per murder. But once the crew fulfilled them, it would turn on those who took out the contract. The contractors were weak, Preacher figured, because they had to rely on outsiders to do their dirty work.

Heatley grew up in Harlem on 144th Street, and the fact that he had oratorical skills is remarkable, given that he only went as far as the third grade in school. Preacher's life from that point followed the familiar pattern of a young kid born poor in the ghetto. By his own admission, Preacher was hustling on the street, peddling heroin, and committing burglaries and armed robberies. He also learned the martial arts and could take care of himself in a street fight.

By the time Preacher had grown up, he was 6'5" tall, stocky, and a real charmer, who knew how to finesse a situation. When his face lit up in a disarming smile, you could almost forget that he was a stone cold killer whom many law enforcement officials had labeled a "psychopath." According to Preacher, he led a quiet life. "I didn't hang on corners, even though I owned most of the stores around Dunbar," he told F.E.D.S. magazine. Preacher recruited John Cuff , a brother as colorless as Preacher was charismatic, to serve as his "Merchant of Death." Slender and gangly, Cuff, who was known as "Big Cuz" on the street, was a city housing cop from 1981 until 1986. He grew up with some of the Preacher Crew members. In 1986, Cuff left the police force to become the Preacher's right hand man. Cuff acted as Preacher's bodyguard and driver.

Preacher ordered Cuff to lure Anthony (Malik) Boatwright, one of his top henchmen, to the basement of his apartment building. Preacher thought that Boatwright was becoming too big within his organization and hence a potential rival. He knew Boatwright was as ruthless as he was because he had helped mutilate and murder a 12-year-old boy.

On March 21, 1994, Boatwright came to Preacher's apartment; Preacher, Cuff and two of his crew took him to the basement. Boatwright was relaxed and joking when suddenly two of the Preacher's men jumped him and held him down while Cuff pulled out a gun and shot Boatwright in the head. Cuff supervised as his accomplices proceeded to cut up Boatwright's body with a circular saw. Cuff then burned off the tattoos on Boatwright's arms and head and tossed his body parts into an abandoned building in Harlem.

The authorities believe the Preacher Crew committed dozens of murders in the basement. On one occasion, the psychos shared a champagne toast to celebrate one of the killings. Preacher kept his crew under strict control, and some reports have compared his gang to a cult. He forbade his members from using drugs, fighting with each other, or stealing money from the crew. Members knew that they would end up in the basement of Preacher's apartment if they broke the rules. To make sure his crew got the message, he regularly beat and lashed them with a belt.

The authorities had no luck getting Preacher—Harlem's most violent gangster—off the street. Still, they doggedly pursued the investigation, hoping to find an informant within the Preacher Crew. Eventually, Preacher's cold-blooded style of leadership did help the investigation. Preacher was eliminating members of his crew, including some longtime associates who had fallen out of favor. Fearing he might be next, one of the crew members went to police and asked for protection. He began to reveal the inside workings of the Preacher Crew, including the details of its infamous killing chamber.

It took more than five years, but in August 1996, the US Attorney's Office for the Southern District of New York drew up a 47-count indictment charging Heatley, Cuff, and 16 crew members with drug trafficking, 11 murders and 11 murder conspiracies. On August 12, 1996, several members of the Joint Organized Crime Task Force of the FBI and NYPD set out to several locations to find Heatley and Cuff and arrest them. They spotted the Preacher on the Grand Concourse at about

3:00 p.m. After watching him make a call from a pay phone, the authorities moved in and put the gangster under arrest, taking him to the 32nd Precinct for booking. Cuff was also arrested and brought to the 32nd Precinct, where he was put in a holding cell with Heatley.

FBI agents began interrogating Preacher, and it was not long before the suspect began asking them if he could help himself by cooperating. The agents did not promise Preacher a cooperative agreement, but they told him that if they did work out a deal, the only thing the federal government would ask of him was to tell the truth. Four days later, Andrew Shapiro, the Legal Aid counsel assigned to defend Heatley, told Sharon McCarthy, the Assistant US Attorney for the Southern District, that his client was willing to cooperate. Shapiro discussed with McCarthy the information Preacher could provide in a number of homicides. On August 21, Preacher signed a cooperative agreement.

But at various points in the meetings, the authorities felt Preacher was lying. because the Information the prosecutor was receiving from other informants was contradicting Preacher's statements. Prosecutors finally told Preacher they did not need his cooperation and proceeded to indict him in November 1996 on racketeering, drug trafficking and nine murder charges. If Preacher was convicted, the federal government would seek the death penalty.

Preacher had no intention of going to trial and taking the chance of getting the death penalty. He decided to follow the recent tradition of the "tough" Harlem gangster turned snitch and began singing like the proverbial canary. In February 1996, he finally worked out a deal with federal prosecutors and pled guilty to federal racketeering charges, including his role in 13 murders. In return, he was sentenced to life in prison, or more specifically, life plus 225 years. Three months later, Cuff pled guilty to federal charges, acknowledging that as a Preacher Crew member, he had killed 10 people.

Cuff escaped the chair, but would spend the rest of his life in prison. At the plea hearing, Cuff admitted to participating in the murder of members of both the Preacher Crew and those of rival groups. On one occasion, Cuff calmly corrected the government's version of events. "Mr. Cuff shot a man twice in the head," Prosecutor Sharon McCarthy told the court. "Not true," said Cuff. "I twisted his neck and choked him."

All eighteen members of the Preacher Crew were convicted and sent to jail. Federal prosecutors said the Preacher Crew committed 40 homicides for sure, but that the number was probably higher. In January 1997, police spokesman Lieutenant Dennis Cirillo revealed that the Preacher Crew investigation had led to the closing of 70 homicide cases in Harlem's 32nd precinct. A chilling chapter in New York City history had come to an end.

TWENTY

Michael Harris: A Convicted Drug Kingpin Who Gave One of America's Most Respected Actors His Start on Broadway

Michael "Harry-O" Harris

THE STREET HUSTLER who wants to go legit is as well worn a cliché as you are likely to find in the annals of criminal lore. It also happens to be based in truth. Many gangsters throughout history have invested money in legitimate businesses. While some do this simply as a money laundering front, others do so with the hopes of finally and completely transitioning over into the straight world. While the instincts that serve one well in the streets rarely work in the "real" world, some gangsters do have legitimate business savvy that can be applied in other areas. The proliferation of the cocaine trade throughout the 1980s gave many enterprising hustlers a chance to finance their dreams. One nearly made it.

Michael Harris was born on September 20th, 1960, on West 46th Street in South Central Los Angeles. He was raised is a single parent household by a hardworking mother. She had two jobs, leaving her with very little time to watch over her son. Michael's father, who he described as a "wealthy businessman with three families," left when the he was just five years old. His mother tried hard to make sure that he had a semblance of a normal family life, as well as an alternative to what the increasingly dangerous streets of south central had to offer. She helped to send him to West Los Angeles community college.

Unfortunately, her vision was not to be. This was the turbulent 1960s. Machinations were already underway that would affect Michael's young adulthood. Racial and economic tensions were reshaping the public consciousness. The civil rights movement was well underway, with the black power movement soon to follow. In the black working class city of Oakland, The Black Panther Party for Self Defense was born. The party would have a profound influence on black youth nationwide, especially in cities along the West Coast. They influenced many ghetto youths to politicize and organize. As the sixties transitioned into the seventies, the Panthers were weakened through infighting and assaults by various government agencies.

Various street gangs in Los Angeles, once inspired by the Panthers, began to step into the void that was left. They became more militaristic and organized their feuds more plentiful and bloody. Soon, pretty much every black gang in L.A. claimed affiliation with either the Bloods or the Crips. While under that banner, they identified with their neighborhood of origin, splitting into various sets or "factions." Michael Harris became affiliated with a Blood set known as the Bounty Hunters.

In the 1970s, America began a love affair with cocaine. Popularized by the disco scene, cocaine was seen as something of a lavish indulgence, relegated to the rich. In the 1980s, a cheaper, smoke able version known as crack made te drug accessible to the poorer classes. South Central was ground zero for the crack explosion, and Michael Harris was in a position to capitalize. He began selling cocaine with his younger brother David and became what fellow bloods might have referred to as a "Baller," or a fellow gang member who strikes it rich in the drug trade.

Harris lorded over a drug empire that supplied cocaine to many states across the U.S., including Los Angeles, Texas and New York. He was so adept at moving the product that Columbian suppliers were encouraged to deal with him directly. At age 26, Michael "Harry-O" Harris was a millionaire.

At this point, Harris decided it was time to leave the drug business behind and pursue more legitimate goals. He began to invest in real estate and various businesses. He owned a 20 fleet limousine service, hair salons, an exotic car dealership and a construction company. Harris also seemed to have an affinity for the entertainment industry. He produced a play called Stepping into Tomorrow that featured the daughters of slain black leaders Martin Luther King and Malcolm X, as well as the daughters of Harry Bellafonte and Sidney Poitier. He also produced a Broadway play called Checkmates, which featured Ruby Dee, Paul Winnfield and an up and coming star named Denzel Washington.

Washington, a native of Mount Vernon, New York, had already developed quite a resume by the time Checkmates

Denzel Washington and Michael 'Harry-O' Harris in their younger days.

premiered on Broadway. He was known for playing Dr. Phillip Chandler on the acclaimed hospital drama St. Elsewhere. He had been nominated for a best actor Oscar for Cry Freedom. Checkmates was his Broadway debut, adding to what had already been shaping up to be a stellar career.

Checkmates was also a landmark in a very different sense. Michael Harris, gang-member and cocaine kingpin, was the first African American to produce a Broadway show. This milestone might have been more celebrated had it not been for his previous occupation. The fact that he was arrested as Checkmates premiered on Broadway certainly didn't help matters at all.

Harris was charged with narcotics distribution and attempted murder. He was convicted on the attempted murder charge (which has since been recanted) in 1987, and has since been serving a 28-year sentence in San Quinton maximum security prison. His entrepreneurial spirit did not die in prison. In fact, he is probably better known to the public as the man who put up $1.5 million in seed money for a fledgling gangster rap label called Death Row Records. Death Row went on to become one of the most storied and infamous labels in music history. Though Harris was not able to partake in any of the spoils, his wife won a $106 million lawsuit against the label in 2005, sending it into bankruptcy.

Denzel Washington, of course, is now one of the most popular and respected actors in cinema history. He has made a career of roles that present positive and powerful images of black manhood (his Oscar-winning turn in Training Day being a rare exception to that rule). He met Michael Harris through the limousine company that he owned, which is how he ended up scoring the role in Checkmates. It would not be unreasonable to conclude that Denzel had no idea of Michael's real occupation at the time, since it surely would not have been in his best interest to advertise his status as a major cocaine dealer.

Had Michael Harris been allowed to complete his transition into the entertainment business, there is no telling what he could have accomplished. Perhaps there would have been more productions starring Mr. Washington. Alas, the drug game is not known for allowing an easy exodus. Harris likely knew that going in. He has received parole and is currently awaiting release. Meanwhile, Denzel Washington is likely signing on for a role in another blockbuster and making space on his shelf for another award.

TWENTY ONE

The Rock: How One of Rap's Most Gifted Producers Ran Afoul of Some Thugs From the Home Town

Peter Philips aka "Pete Rock"

AS ANY COP or crook will tell you, the criminal element is volatile by nature. It comes with the territory. Those who live by an illegal means have a penchant for taking advantage of weakness. When trying to transition over into the legit world, they often have trouble shedding their old ways. New opportunities to enter the "straight" world are often squandered and bridges are burned.

No people feel the sting of betrayal more than those who extend a helping hand to criminals looking to reform. Kindness is mistaken for weakness, and the Good Samaritan receives a slap in the face for his efforts. All parties involved would probably have been better off had they just stayed in their own lanes. The straight world, like the underworld, is not for everybody.

One gifted rap music producer had to learn this the hard way.

Mount Vernon New York, a city in Westchester County that borders the borough of the Bronx, was a veritable hot bed of black music talent in the late 1980s and early 1990s. The mostly black town birthed a number of celebrities from Heavy D to Denzel Washington.

Notable among them was rap DJ and producer Pete Rock. After serving a tenure on the legendary Marley Marls WBLS radio show, "In Control With Marley Marl," Rock teamed up with Mount Vernon rapper CL Smooth and released the hip-hop classic Mecca & The Soul Brother. Though not a sales behemoth, the album is/was widely regarded as an artistic high point for rap music. Pete quickly became one of the most requested producers of that time period, mostly on strength of his jazzy, horn laden beats. After he and CL signed a deal with Elektra Records, Pete began to taking steps to introduce more talent from Money Earnin. Mount Vernon to the rest of the world.

Among Pete's many prospects was The YG'z, which was short for "Young Gunz." The YG'z were known by many to be one of Mount Vernon's most notorious street gangs, as it's membership consisted largely of local thugs. Regardless of their reputation, Pete went to great pains to help them realize their music industry dreams. They were featured on the song "Death Becomes You," which appeared on the soundtrack to the film, Menace II Society.

That same year, they released a seven song EP titled Street Nigga. Six of the seven songs were produced by none other than Pete Rock himself. The first single, which also happened to the title song, was released to little fanfare. The EP itself was met with poor reviews. These factors, coupled with the group's penchant for thuggish behavior, caused Pete to gradually disassociate from them. However, severing ties with the YG'z would prove much harder than anticipated.

In the summer of 1993, at the Mount Vernon Family Day Picnic, both Pete and The YG'z were in attendance. Combat Jack, a writer for hip-hop website www.byroncrawford.com was in attendance as well. On March 25, 2005, Combat Jack wrote a detailed account of events that supposedly took place at the picnic. Supposedly, Pete was assaulted by members of the YG'z while talking to a young woman. They approached him and demanded his attention. When he obliged, a YG'z member subsequently sucker punched him, knocking him unconscious and sprawled out on a picnic blanket. While incapacitated, the YG'z allegedly rifled through his pockets and robbed him.

Upon regaining consciousness, Pete was said to have left the event in great haste. The incident was never reported to the authorities by either Pete or anyone else in attendance. In the same article, Combat Jack said these events repeated themselves at a black tie music industry event he also attended.

Pete Rock himself, however, remembers things quite differently, as noted by the UK hip-hop publication Hip-Hop Connection. According to Pete, he merely had a physical altercation with a friend who was trying to embarrass him in front of the crowd. After knocking the man down, Pete claimed he ran to escape the authorities. Pete said that the man was not a member of the YG'z but, in fact, was a childhood acquaintance that has since passed on. He seemed remorseful. His version of events did not include the YG'z at all.

Aside from these two accounts, neither side has anyone to collaborate their story. The incident was never officially reported, so there is no way to substantiate either side. Since that picnic, rumors have persisted all throughout Mount Vernon. With every retelling of events, the story grows more elaborate and intricate. It became part of local hip-hop folklore. Interestingly, more people are perhaps familiar with the many stories surrounding this incident than with any of the YG'z music. At the other end of the spectrum, Pete Rock is known mostly for his artistic output.

In the years following the incident, Pete Rock and CL Smooth parted ways. Pete Rock continued to produce music for well known rappers such as Nas, Public Enemy, Heavy D, and the Notorious B.I.G. He continues to release albums to this day. Though the style of rap music production he pioneered is no longer in favor, he maintains a small but loyal following among East Coast hip-hop traditionalists.

The YG'z, on the other hand, have completely faded into Hip-Hop obscurity. They were dropped from Elektra, never to release an LP. The Street Nigga EP is now a forgotten relic of hardcore rap. The era of gangbanging they represented soon gave way to the proliferation of L.A. street gangs that began infiltrating the jails and streets of New York City throughout the remainder of the 1990s. The black music scene in Mount Vernon also diminished, though its contributions have not been forgotten.

Pete Rock aka The "Chocolate Boy Wonder" learned the hard way that his musical talents and general good will would be better suited to those who are deserving of it. The YG'z learned that the extortion and strong arm tactics cultivated in the streets do not play well in the legitimate world.

Real world gangsterism, unlike its musical counterpart, has consequences. Having real gangsters making gangster music might seem like the perfect match to outsiders, but those in the industry know better. Street knowledge and the ability to be a successful criminal can never compensate for true talent.

TWENTY TWO

Spare Change: How a Modern Day Desperado Died by the Gun but Managed to Live on Through Rap Music

Kelvin "Fifty Cent" Martin

LIKE MANY YOUNG people that grew up in Southside Queens during the 1990s, Curtis Jackson was enamored with the drug culture he saw around him, or rather the material accoutrements that came with it. The creature comforts and fetish items of a successful drug dealer were something to strive for, but the pitfalls of the dope game were hardly worth the headache.

Ever the enterprising young man, Curtis saw the burgeoning rap industry as a more than viable alternative, seeing as how rappers lived longer and had less of a chance of going to jail. As he began to piece together his rap persona, he realized that he would need a moniker that was larger than life. As was/is the tradition, he looked to the underworld culture that fueled his aspirations. His search led him to the Borough of Brooklyn, where a fearless stick-up artist made a name by preying on rappers, dealers and just about anyone else who crossed his path.

During the 1980s, one of the most fabled "stick-up kids" in New York was Kelvin "50 Cent" Martin. Supposedly named "50 Cent" because no amount of money was too minuscule for him to overlook (or perhaps due to his very loose affiliation with the 5% Nation), Martin was a one man crime wave. His methods and attitude harkened back to the desperadoes of the old west, making him notorious throughout New York's biggest borough. Dealers, rappers and even civilians were weary of him.

Born on July 24, 1964, Kelvin Martin was raised primarily by his grandmother Irene Martin and spent a good deal of his childhood in a Puerto Rican neighborhood in the Bronx. As he entered his teenage years, Kelvin Martin's stomping ground was the R.V. Ingersoll Houses and Walt Whitman Houses in Fort Greene, Brooklyn, known to many as the Fort Greene Projects.

The 50 cents legend is enhanced by his diminutive size. At 5'2 tall and 120 lbs, Martin was hardly physically imposing, but his attitude and propensity for gun play made him ten feel tall. Though reportedly not much of a street fighter, he made up for his lack of hand skills in other ways. Armed with two long barrel revolvers (a .357 Magnum and a Colt .45) and a bullet proof vest, he prowled city streets ready for war and looking for potential marks. Even without his guns, Martins brazen and cocky nature was uncommon even for the time. Driving his willingness to shoot first and ask questions later was an alertness and awareness that boarded on paranoia.

Kelvin inevitably ended up doing a stint on Riker's Island in the Juvenile Detention center on the C74 block sometime during the mid 1980s, where future Hip-Hop entrepreneur Jimmy "Henchman" Rosemond caught wind of his reputation. Upon his release, Martin returned to the Fort Greene housing projects and linked up with the infamous Supreme Team (different from the similarly named crew stationed in Jamaica Queens), where he was mentored in the ways of the streets by the Supreme Team member "Rap".

Martin would take his bounty of "Dookie Jewelry" down to New York's City's famed "Diamond District" on 47th Street. There, he would attempt to sell them to fences such as "One Arm" Monk or other jewelry store owners.

Though Martin preyed on rap artists, he actually had many associates and friends in the Hip-Hop world. Among them was Eric Barrier, better known as DJ Eric B. of the rap duo Eric B. & Rakim. In fact, Martin appeared in a photo on the back of the duo's classic debut Paid in Full, crouched beside Barrier and decked out in truck jewelry. Oddly, he was rumored to have robbed Rakim for a gold pendant and L.L. Cool J for a gold rope. Though neither story was ever substantiated, they added to his already considerable legend.

Martin ran afoul of more than a few fellow "street legends", among them was a hustler named "Damencio". Martin and Damencio got into a physical altercation at the Empire skating rink. Damencio appeared to be the victor, until deep razor blade wounds began opening up on his face immediately after the two had been separated. Martin had sliced up his face with a razor,

The legendary photo from the back cover of Eric B & Rakim's classic rap album Paid in Full with Kelvin "50 Cent" Martin appearing in the bottom left corner.

but immediately denied any involvement in the situation. Those who know Martin say they have no idea what lead to the incident. Nonetheless, such actions made Martin's list of enemies longer than anyone could comprehend.

50's reign of terror created an atmosphere that made Brooklyn unlivable for him. With his enemies constantly at the ready, they offered him no rest. When Albany projects no longer provided ample protection, Martin joined the United States Armed Forces and took a sabbatical from the streets of Brooklyn. His sabbatical proved short lived, as he was dishonorably discharged in Fort Benning, Georgia, when a robbery warrant came back to haunt him. Shortly after his return, he survived a shooting attempt at the Albee Square Mall. This marked a change in his personality. His outlook became more fatalistic.

Martin again sought solace in the Albany Housing Projects. On October 20, 1987 at around 10 p.m., Kelvin "50 Cent Martin" was found laying on 7th floor stairwell, bleeding from multiple gunshot wounds. He was taken to Brooklyn Kings County hospital, where he was kept in ICU until his condition improved. After being moved from ICU, he suddenly took a turn for the worse and eventually died at the age of 23. Martin, who had been shot over 20 times on nine different occasions in his lifetime, had finally succumbed to the way of the gun. His assailant was Julio "Wemo" Acevedo, who had performed the hit under duress because his family was being held hostage.

Curtis Jackson, better known to rap fans as 50 Cent, is one of the most prosperous and prominent artists of his generation. He has acknowledged the debt he owes to Kelvin Martin, the "original 50 Cent", having openly admitted that it was Kelvin Martin who inspired the name. 50's worldwide fame has lead to people from all over seeking out information regarding the inspiration behind his stage name. That has inevitably lead to the legend of Kelvin Martin having a longer shelf life than it would have otherwise enjoyed. Through the legitimately earned fame of Curtis Jackson, the infamy of Kelvin Martin lives on.

TWENTY THREE

Larry Hoover—Chairman of the Board of the U.S. Prison System

Larry Hoover

IN THE EARLY 1990s, the Gangster Disciples (GDs) were perhaps the most powerful gang in America, even though Larry Hoover, the GDs self-described "Chairman" was serving a 150 to 200-year sentence in prison for a 1973 murder conviction. The fact that Hoover had been incarcerated for nearly two decades did not stop him from becoming the most powerful gangster ever to operate behind bars.

It was widely accepted that the chairman had worked out a deal with prison officials. The "arrangement" gave him wide latitude in every area of his incarceration: what he could eat and wear, who could visit him and how he could interact with the outside community, In 1981, Hoover sent a directive to his gang: No GD was to attack, threaten or disrespect a correctional officer without his approval. Do so and the result would be severe punishment. In return, prison officials transferred Hoover to the Vienna Correctional facility, which sources invariably describe as "college-like campus." In 1987 Hoover's prison status was quietly changed from high security to minimum security.

The GDs has about 8000 to 9000 members behind bars, a veritable army, ready to do the Chairman's bidding. So he could have created a lot of trouble, if he wanted to.

The GDs' sophisticated hierarchy and structure had two board of directors: one for gang members on the outside and one in the prison system. With a total membership of 18,000 to 25,000, the GDs were operating by the early 1990s in 19 out of the 25 police districts and in every neighborhood in the city of Chicago, as well as several Chicago suburbs and the cities of Milwaukee and Madison in Wisconsin.

The GDS trafficked in narcotics big-time and were known for their ruthlessness. Police said the gang was responsible for at least 80 murders annually. Piss of the gang and you could receive a beating —a so-called "pumpkin head." "It is a particularly brutal form of punishment," explained Rick Barrett, a retired DEA agent who investigated Hoover and the GDs. "The GDs put the victim on the ground and tap him on both sides of the head with a baseball bat. The head swells up grotesquely… just like a pumpkin."

By 1993 Hoover, had reached the zenith of his power. "It was during 1993 that Hoover's clout and momentum was the heaviest," explained DEA agent Rick Barrett. "That's when the push was hot and heavy to get him out of prison. Hoover had tried to change his image, but it didn't work. When Hoover went up for his parole hearing, he knew we were on to him."

When Hoover went up before the parole board in March 1993, the Illinois Prison Review Board had received a petition of 5,000 signatures supporting his release. It created the impression that a ground swell in Chicago was building for Hoover's parole petition. Two professors, Dr. Clemens Bertollas of the University of Northern Iowa in Cedar Falls, and Dwight Conquergood of Northwestern University in Evanston, Illinois, wrote op-ed pieces and spoke on his behalf at his parole hearing on Hoover's behalf.

Many politicians, businessmen and political leaders also came to support Hoover's at his parole hearing. The Illinois Prison Review Board was not impressed, and it rejected Hoover's parole application, the 14th time the Chairman's petition had been denied.

The authorities decided to go after Hoover, even though he was in prison. But as a student of organized crime history, Hoover knew how the Feds got John Gotti, the Dapper Don. "They, they, bugged his, his office, they bugged his car," Hoover stammered during one phone call. "They bugged the phone booth, 'cause they knew, knew where he was at."

With the prison was in the southern most part of the state, Getting to it was not easy. Yet gang bangers made the six-hour car drive from Chicago regularly. Prison logs showed that Hoover's visitors were often gang members who used aliases. The trip was a small price to pay for caution. Rather than talk with gang members in the visitor's room, Hoover could move around the grounds, away from any hidden microphones, and to areas where he could do gang business without fear of being bugged.

In early 1993, investigators finally got a break when they busted Charles "Jello" Banks, a charming chubby GD, who got caught selling drugs to an undercover agent working with the police. Investigators saw an opportunity and pressured Banks to cooperate. Facing several years in prison, he agreed to sing for a reduced sentence. Jello had never met the Chairman, but he knew how the gang operated and how it was structured, from the chairman and board of directors down to the soldiers on the street.

The authorities needed probable cause to go up on the wire at Vienna. But until Jello flipped, they had no evidence that could give them that authority. Now they could monitor Larry's private conversations.

In acquiring the legal authority, prosecutors had jumped one barrier, but where were they going to hide the bugs? Hoover didn't stay put, so putting it in usual places—the wall clock, ashtrays or coke machine-- would not work.

DEA agent Rick Barrett was racking his brain, trying to figure out a solution when, one day, an agent he supervised came by his office. The agent was livid with anger and frustration about the way a federal prosecutor was handling an unrelated case. Barrett noticed that the agent was still wearing the visitor's tag from the prosecutor's office. To break the tension, Barrett quipped: "You better watch what you say. Everything is getting back to the prosecutor through his visitor's badge."

A light bulb went off in Barrett's head. Is there a microphone and transmitter small enough to fit into a Vienna prison visitor's badge? he wondered. Barrett was snowed under with work, but he did some digging. He could not find a company that sold such a tiny device, but he did find one in Florida that was willing to develop one for $2500 a pop. Now the Chairman could walk around the prison yard all he wanted, but if the bug worked, investigators would hear everything when he got down, confidential and up close with a visitor.

Ron Safer, the Assistant U.S. Attorney assigned to the Hoover investigation, went to meet with the Deputy Director of the Illinois Corrections system to present the plan and get his approval and cooperation. Given the power of Hoover and his corrupting influence, the authorities decided to select only one prison guard to work with the task force. He was ordered not to breathe a word about the bugging scheme. "Only two of the so called visitor passes were fitted with the bug," Barrett recalled. "All of the others were placebos, meaning they were not equipped with any electronics. They were worn by 'normal' visitors.

Beginning in October, 1993, 350 miles away from Vienna in a federal office in Chicago, the prosecutors began listening in on Hoover's conversations. It was not easy to do. Larry Hoover stuttered; the tape had background noise; the Chairman and his visitors often spoke in street slang; and he liked to move around. Several team members took a stab at translating the tapes.

The investigators present the evidence to a federal grand jury. At dawn on August 31, 1995, law enforcement officials, armed with warrants for the arrest of 38 GD leaders and one cop, moved to take down the leadership of Chicago's most powerful gang. About 250 police and federal agents fanned out through Chicago's Southside and made arrests. A 50 count indictment accused Larry Hoover of masterminding the GDs from his prison cell. The indictments sought the forfeiture of $10 million.

It took two trials but on May 9, 1997, the jury reached a verdict after deliberating for 12 hours. Hoover and the other five defendants were found guilty of participating in a drug conspiracy. At his hearing on June 18, 1998, Hoover, wearing a white undershirt, light tan pants and the laceless shoes of a prisoner, finally stood before a judge. But Hoover still wielded an aura of power. Federal authorities had to fly him in for the hearing because they did not want to risk a roadside ambush.

A SWAT team, dressed in full riot gear, escorted Hoover into the packed courthouse. The judge sentenced Hoover to a mandatory life sentence. He would have to serve the sentence on top of the 150 to 200 year Illinois state sentence he received in 1973.

Hoover's conviction was hailed as the most significant since Al Capone's takedown. "It is the single most important victory in the government's war against organized crime in years," wrote Richard Lindberg, Chicago crime historian. "A criminal enterprise of such staggering proportions is no longer just a street gang. It is the new face of organized crime in a changing world. We better just get use to it."

TWENTY FOUR

Life Imitates Art: How a Rapper Incriminated Himself Through His Music

Aneraen Veshaugn Brown aka "X-Raided"

THOUGH ITS MYSTIQUE has largely subsided in recent years, Gangster Rap was once thought to be a fairly authentic representation of what was going on in America's streets. It drew the ire of politicians and parents groups that saw it as a direct affront to the innocence of its young fanbase. While many gangster rappers had little to no experience with what they rapped about, there were some that did. One Sacramento rapper tailored his songs a little too close to his own reality, to the point where he ended up incurring the wrath of the law.

Anerae Veshaughn Brown was an aspiring rap artist who went by the name X-Raided. He had ties to the Garden Blocc Crips. While recording his debut, the Garden Blocc Crips and the Meadowview Bloods were engaged in a street war. Being in the midst of such circumstances had an effect on Browns work. As per gangsta rap parlance, he became a "street reporter." His songs were filled with his thoughts and experiences.

X-Raided released his debut album Psycho Active in 1992. The cover art that accompanied the album was provocative indeed. It showed X-Raided pointing a .38 caliber revolver to his head. The lyrical content proved more provocative still. This hardly made Psycho Active stand out in the market place as such shock tactics were fast becoming de rigueur for gangster music. What did make Psycho Active stand out are the events that informed the cover of the LP as well as its subject matter. These events came back to haunt Brown, as he was arrested the day before his album hit stores.

In March of 1992, Patricia Harris was murdered by armed gang members who raided her home. She was the grandmother of two members of the Meadowview Bloods. Five people were subsequently arrested for the murder, including Brown. While rappers getting arrested for violent crimes might seem like old news today, in the early 1990s it was still relatively new. Brown likely did not anticipate that the arrest would boost his "street credibility," as that had yet to become the quality by which gangster rappers were measured. What he also probably had not anticipated is that his own music would be used to incriminate him.

A track from the album entitled "Still Shooting" described a home invasion in vivid detail that bore a close resemblance to the murder of Patricia Harris. On the song, X-Raided rapped: "I'm killin' moms, daddys and nephews. I'm killin' sons, daughters and sparin' you." As if that was not enough, the Revolver shown on the album cover was believed by authorities to be the murder weapon. While the gun was never retrieved or proven to have been used in the murder, X-Raided was arrested and sentenced to 31 years in prison for first degree murder and gang-related homicide.

Perhaps the earliest proponent of the "Stop Snitching" code, Brown never testified. He admitted to being present during the murder but denied being the triggerman. "I could have testified and gone home, but I kept it real," Brown boasted. He clearly saw this decision as an honorable one.

Incarceration did not deter Browns career as a rap artist. If anything he became more prolific behind bars. From 1992 to 1995 he recorded what would be his second album, Xorcist, while in the Sacramento County Jail. The album was released on December 12,, 1995. The album was recorded entirely over the phone, as X-Raided could not get to a studio and had no access to state of the art recording equipment. The sound quality was poor, but X-Raided fans still got what they wanted.

His third album, Unforgiven, was completed under fairly extraordinary circumstances. This time out, X-Raided was aided by a guard who served as an intermediary between the rapper and his label Black Market Records. The correction officer delivered messages, beats and completed tracks to both X-Raided and the label. The risk taking paid off, as the album had better sound quality than its predecessor and managed to chart on Billboard following its release on April 20, 1999. X-Raided was proving to be quite irrepressible behind bars.

X-Raided again proved to be quite resourceful while recording vocals for his fourth set, Vengeance Is Mine. This time he used a DAT recorder that he procured through illegal means. The officer who smuggled in the recording device was terminated. X-Raided confessed that the officer had aided him. Regardless of the casualties, Brown continued his recording career. Browns musical catalog grew substantially throughout the 2000s, consisting of numerous studio albums and compilations.

Brown also became a staunch defender of West Coast gangsta rap and the perceived East Coast bias harbored by major hip-hop publications such as The Source Magazine. He felt that East Coast rappers who indulged in the same violent subject matter as him were shown blatant favoritism. He even went so far as to accuse the publication of accepting payola in exchange for favorable album reviews. Though he could not profit from his album sales, he seemed to exhibit a sincere dedication to his craft.

Even behind bars, X-Raided could not avoid drama. In May of 2010, X-Raided was stabbed during a prison riot at Pleasant Valley State Prison. He was attacked by an inmate wielding a toothbrush adorned with eight razor blades. The inmates that attacked him were affiliated with the Northern Riders gang. It is rumored that the inmates were trying to get Brown to release and produce an album by them. When Brown refused, they opted for making a name for themselves by taking him out. All are now facing attempted murder charges. Brown survived the stabbing and will undoubtedly continue to release new material.

It is not uncommon for one to become more productive and focused while incarcerated. Inmates often find religion, become voracious readers, and workout obsessively in an attempt to fill time. When said productivity allows an inmate to seemingly prosper from a violent reputation, priorities can become twisted. While X-Raided's status as a convict and murderer may add to his mystique, it does not erase the fact that a grandmother became a casualty in a gang war. X-Raided can continue to release albums, but the revenues generated will be of little consolation to the family of Patricia Harris.

TWENTY FIVE

How A Legendary Lyricist May Have Unwittingly Helped A Los Angeles Street Gang Invade His Hometown

DJ Kay Gee, Treach and Vin Rock of the rap group Naughty By Nature

THOUGH STREET GANGS and gang violence existed long before the inception of hip-hop culture, many believe there is an inextricable link between the two. While it is true that hip-hop has its roots in the aftermath of the Bronx street gang wars of the 1970s, the culture has since outgrown those beginnings and gone on to accommodate and represent much more than gang affiliations. However, within the subsets of gangster and hardcore rap exist a contingent of rappers who define themselves by such affiliations and use them to enhance their images. Some do so unwittingly, allowing gang bangers to become part of their entourages, as they tour around the country. One popular rap group of the early 1990s did just that with a notorious Los Angeles street gang.

Naughty By Nature burst onto the scene in 1991 with the smash hit "O.P.P." The song became a sensation, getting constant spins on MTV and radio stations across the country. The song, as well as the album on which it appeared, would soon attain platinum status. Treach, the group's front man, became a star in his own right. His rapid fire lyrical delivery made him stand out from other rappers of the day. His hardcore themes and thuggish appearance instantly placed him as one of the harder edged artists around at the time despite the relatively "happy" party anthems he was known for. The group collectively put their hometown of East Orange, New Jersey on the hip-hop map.

By 1993, the group was touring in support of its second album 19 Naughty III and their second top ten single "Hip-Hop Hooray." On a summer's day that year, the group's tour bus pulled into their hometown. Among their considerable entourage were two aspiring rap artists by the name of True G and Love Child. Neither was a native of East Orange or even the eastern United States, for that matter. They both hailed from Inglewood, California, and were, in fact, members of the notorious Queens Street Blood set that resided there. They stepped off the tour bus wearing colors that advertised their affiliation. During a cookout that took place that week, the two began preaching Bloods gospel to the teenagers in attendance.

The kids of East Orange were no stranger to gangs. Prior to the arrival of these two mysterious visitors, the town had had its fair share. However, those factions were numerous and scattered without a hint of organization. The type of gang activity that proliferated in Los Angeles was something else entirely. The Bloods and Crips emerged from the racial and economic turmoil of the late sixties and early seventies to become L.A's dominant black street gangs. Both groups use colors as signifiers: Bloods wear blue and Crips wear red. They also identify themselves by their neighborhood of origin. Their bloody turf wars were the stuff of legend, and the onset of the crack era only escalated things. Throughout the 80s they began to infiltrate other cities across the U.S. At the same time, the emerging West Coast gangsta rap scene, as well as various movies, mythologized their exploits.

Being a gang member, or having gang members in your inner circle, would be a significant boost to one's street credibility and that reality was not lost on the popular rap artists of the time. Many West Coast rappers had openly claimed membership in various sets in their music as well as in interviews. East Coast rappers, who at the time were still somewhat ignorant of the phenomenon, began using older and more experienced Los Angeles gang members (also known as O.G's or Original Gangsters) as bodyguards and guides when doing shows on the West Coast. As West Coast gangsta rap increased in popularity and notoriety, certain East Coast rappers went further in terms of embracing and adapting to it. They began to develop significant ties out west. It is likely some West Coast rappers saw these relationships as beneficial, since East Coast rappers sometimes had better and more direct access to major record labels whose main offices were in New York City.

The kids of East Orange, likely primed by all of the West Coast gangsta rap they had devoured up until that point, where enthralled. They were hearty candidates. That True G and Love

Child were not prominent Bloods members back home did not matter. Either way, the kids of East Orange were intrigued. Likely not having any better prospects in terms of employment or family support systems, they decided to join up. A name was concocted that would emphasize the hybrid nature of this new set: "Double ii." One "I" stood for Inglewood, California, while the other stood for "Illtown," which was the nickname for East Orange.

The set firmly established itself on 15th and Williams streets. Determined to live up to the deadly reputation popularized by their counterparts in L.A., the Double ii Bloods wasted no time in making their presence known across the town. Bloods graffiti and slogans would soon adorn walls everywhere. Red bandannas and clothing became the required uniforms for many. Blood doctrine became second nature. Members were expected to know the history of the gang as well as the many slang terms that populated its language and customs. The number 550 was code for civilian. Dispensing of an enemy was known as "putting in work."

Anthony Criss aka "Treach" of Naughty By Nature

East Orange has since become a hotbed of gang activity, and Naughty By Nature is nowhere near as popular as they once were. The group members have gone on to other projects, most notably Treach, who has become a presence in B-level action pictures and even in his own soft core porn film. Though the group has never fully endorsed the ii Bloods publicly, certain song titles on their albums are said to contain references to the set (certain instances of the letter i appear as ii). Treach has also taken a staunchly anti-gang stance as of late. He appeared in the anti-gang film Think Twice, Little Gangsta, in 2009.

While it's quite likely that Treach and the other members of Naughty By Nature did not intend to introduce Los Angeles style gangbanging to their hometowns, it is important to remember that such organizations take any opportunity to increase membership and/or territory. It should also be noted that the relationship between criminal organizations and the entertainment industry existed long before rappers began to flaunt such affiliations. Blood and Crip sets now populate every major city in the northeastern United States, which is a very sharp contrast to way things were before the two visitors from Inglewood set foot in East Orange. Though Naughty By Nature have moved on, the Bloods remain a constant presence in East Orange.

TWENTY SIX

Haywood T. Kirkland: A Vietnam Veteran Who Inspired One of the Most Memorable Heist Films of the 90s

Cleon (Bokeem Woodbine), Jose (Freddy Rodriguez), Anthony Curtis (Larenz Tate), and Kirby (Keith David) in a scene fromDead Presidents

WHILE THE HUGHES Brothers movie, Dead Presidents, was not a commercial or critical smash, it attained cult status upon its release in 1995. This was largely due to its eclectic soundtrack full of golden oldies, as well as the Hughes Brothers masterful use of haunting visuals. Among the most mesmerizing of the latter was the image of the protagonists wearing mime-like face paint and brandishing automatic weapons during the climactic, action-packed heist scene.

The image of star Larenz Tate's face made ghostly by black and white paint proved so striking that it was used for the films poster. While the image gave the films third act an air of surrealism, the story and all of its elements were inspired by real life events of a man named Haywood T. Kirkland.

Kirkland grew up in Washington, D.C. He was an unremarkable high school student who loved shooting pool. He got drafted to the United States armed forces and was shipped off to the war In Vietnam. While serving his tour of duty, the racism and atrocities he witnessed had a profound affect on his mindset, and he began developing a radical worldview.

The hostility he suffered at the hands of whites, as well his fellow African Americans, served only to intensify this worldview. "Even my own people said, `You was crazy for going over there in the first place," Kirkland later recalled. "There was no readjustment period for me. I left Vietnam—22 hours later I was back."

Kirkland's efforts to adjust to civilian life proved fruitless. After taking some classes in computer programming, he took a job at the post office. He found it to be not much of a change from the military structure he had become accustomed to in the service. However, he did come about a bit of information that would prove useful. Old, worn money was routinely brought back from European army bases to be destroyed.

Since the money was to be disposed of, Kirkland rationalized that no one would miss it if it were stolen. He figured the segment of society that needed the money most would be put to much better use. "I thought that with some resources, we could do some of the things that we thought was right to do—set up community medical centers and things of that nature," Kirkland said.

On a December morning in 1969, Kirkland and two accomplices approached a mail truck driver while he stood at the loading dock of the Federal Home Loan Bank Board on Indiana Avenue NW in DC. There faces were obscured by ash. One of them was disguised as a postal worker. They stole a bag carrying $382,000 worth of worn out bills. The driver was then instructed to tell police that the robbers all looked alike. He emerged from the robbery unharmed.

Kirkland and his associates were apprehended. At trial, the defense tried to portray them in as sympathetic a light as possible. Kirkland had been generous with his ill gotten gains, doling out money to friends and neighbors. The judge, however, was not moved and sentenced him to 30 years in state prison.

While incarcerated, Haywood found a new calling as an advocate for the rights of incarcerated Vietnam veterans, organizing the Incarcerated Veterans Assistance Organization. At the time, over 25 percent of the inmates incarcerated at Lorton penitentiary had served in the Vietnam War.

He also adopted the name Ari Sesu Merretazon. The name Merretazon comes from an ancient Egyptian dialect and literally translates to "guardian servant chosen to do the will of the creator."

After taking courses at the Antioch school of law, Kirkland successfully appealed his conviction. His efforts to help other inmates played a major role in his early release. He was released from prison in 1975 after serving just 5 years.

He continued to run the Incarcerated Veterans Assistance Organization out of the basement of his home located on Peabody Street NE. in DC He got a job with the Veteran's Administration as a counselor for incarcerated veterans In Little Rock. There, he became an editor at a black newspaper and attained masters in community economic development from New Hampshire College's graduate school of business. After beginning a teaching career in Arkansas, an 18 wheeler demolished his car and he was put into a coma for five days. Upon recovering, he was divinely inspired and started the interfaith Developing Times Ministry.

His life would soon be immortalized in Wallace Terry's book Bloods: Black Veterans of the Vietnam War: an Oral History. Immediately upon its release, Terry was inundated with offers for the rights to his book. None of the offers were to his liking, but then the Hughes brothers came along, expressing special interest in the chapter of Bloods that chronicled the darker period of Kirkland's life. Terry received a significant sum for the rights to the book. Kirkland even served as a technical consultant.

Dead Presidents takes more than a bit of artistic license with the details of Kirkland's story, mostly using it as a jumping off point for a brutal heist film with stylistic and thematic similarities to the old blaxploitation classics. This was not lost on Kirkland, who saw very little of his own story in what eventually made it to the screen.

Still, he was very objective in his assessment of the film. "I didn't make the movie. I am not responsible for the movie. So it's all on the Hughes brothers. . . . Of course, I would have liked to have it have a little more to do with the politics of the time, but that's just armchair quarterbacking right now. I want to support them. They are young, enterprising, talented filmmakers. They're 23 years old—you know? . . . They did a good job. The movie's successful making money and I'm proud of them."

After a rather bumpy start, Haywood T. Kirkland reformed and made a useful place for himself in the world. Criminality was never really in his heart. Unlike Anthony Curtis, the doomed protagonist of Dead Presidents, Kirkland met with a well earned happy ending.

Alas, that is rarely the story that Hollywood likes to tell. The Hughes Brothers have never specialized in films that have particularly optimistic views of human nature. Kirkland isn't complaining though. In their own way, The Hughes brothers have acknowledged the suffering endured by tons of veterans upon returning home. That has got to be worth something.

TWENTY SEVEN

Cocaine Kingdom: How a Crack Empire was Established in Britain

Lincoln White

ORGANIZED CRIME ISN'T exactly one of the first things that come to mind when one thinks of the United Kingdom. Not that the U.K doesn't have it's share of crime and gangsters, but drug kingpins living in the lap of luxury tends to be an image associated with the United States or even South America. Though the U.S. does consume more illegal narcotics than any other nation in the world, it is not the only country with an appetite for drugs. It's also not the only country where a drug dealer can amass a personal fortune to rival that of any corporate CEO. One man in particular found the U.K. to be very fertile territory for the cocaine business.

Lincoln White came to Britain from Jamaica in 1993 and stayed longer than his tourist visa warranted. He eventually ended up dividing time between Britain and his home country. By 2004 he had become the biggest cocaine dealer the United Kingdom had ever seen. He sat atop a drug empire valued at 170 million pounds sterling. He lorded over this empire with a humble demeanor and a keen sense of business.

White imported cocaine mainly from Central and South America, but he had connections all over the globe to ensure that his supply would never run low. In addition to Britain and Jamaica, the Lincoln White cartel operated in Nicaragua, Mexico, The Antilles, Grenada and Panama. At its height, his organization was importing 2 million pounds worth of cocaine a month into the U.K. Once the drug arrived in its powder form, it was taken to a flat in Flapham, South London, where it was cooked up into its crack cocaine variant.

The drug was smuggled in through fairly simple means. Couriers carried the powder in shampoo bottles that were intercepted by another employee of White's upon arrival. Maxine Hemmings, who worked in the duty free area at Gatwick airport, collected the shampoo bottles from couriers before they went through customs.

White had obviously studied the mistakes of many of his predecessors. Successful drug dealers are prone to showing off their wealth. Excessive, lavish lifestyles are par for the course. While such trappings are the main reason many enter the drug business, they attract unwanted attention from law enforcement as well as the government. Lincoln White went against the grain in this regard. While in Britain he resided in a modest apartment for which he paid 1,000 pounds a month. He also drove a modest Peugeot 206.

White did not adhere to the dress code or spending habits of his "Yardie" Jamaican counterparts who favored tacky gold jewelry and loud clothing. Though White did favor designer clothes and expensive cigars, he preferred not to be a walking stereotype or a cop magnet.

Along with his rather low key living situation, he adopted a low key personality. Very often high level professional criminals have personas to match their bank accounts, but White opted for blending into the crowd. He was so reserved you could spot him on the street and not give him a second glance. He did not seem to draw his inspiration from the flamboyant villains of Hollywood films, but rather, preferred to used common sense.

However his lifestyle in his home country stood in sharp contrast to his meager existence in the Queens country. He owned not one but two mansions in Montego Bay, for which he paid cash. The money he earned in Britain stretched far in Jamaica, and it allowed him to spend his time there as though he was on a perpetual vacation.

White maintained the loyalty of his employees by treating them very well, ensuring that they would never do or say anything to jeopardize the operation. Couriers were treated to paid flights and plush hotels where they could lay up for considerable amounts of time. They were even provided with ample spending money for other expenses.

On March 20 and 21 of 2004, British police conducted a series of raids which resulted in ten arrests. It was a massive effort that included 500 officers from the West Yorkshire Police, the Metropolitan Police, the national crime squad and H&M

customs & excise. When the Flapham flat was raided, it turned out to be the biggest cocaine seizure ever in the United Kingdom. Authorities confiscated over 10.9 kilos of powder cocaine.

Lincoln White was arrested in March of 2003 following a 14-month investigation. Following a tip off from an American informant, White was bugged and conversations about drug couriers were caught on tape.

White's trial took place in a South London courthouse where policemen armed with machine guns patrolled the area for its duration. White himself was escorted by the police and even transported via helicopter. Authorities were not taking any chances. The trial lasted for ten weeks, and the jury deliberated for ten days. White was found guilty and sentenced to 25 years in prison.

During sentencing, Judge Edward Southwell took a moment to address what he saw as the unmitigated gall of Lincoln White: "You played for the highest stakes with what I consider to be breathtaking arrogance, and those stakes must now be met." He even as far as to say that he would recommend that White be deported once he had served his sentence. If he does return to his native Jamaica in 2019, he will likely not enjoy the same lifestyle he had before his arrest.

Every criminal thinks they can avoid the mistakes made by others. They think they will be the one that will last and ultimately ride off into the sunset having fooled the authorities. In reality, even the smartest and most cautious crook is only biding his time. The drug game is not designed to be played indefinitely. It has a shelf life and an expiration date. Lincoln White kept his head low and was able to operate unmolested for quite sometime. In the process, he managed to prove that America is not the only place where opportunity can be found.

TWENTY EIGHT

King of Thieves: How a Stick-Up Artist from Brooklyn Became Hip-Hops Answer to Lee Harvey Oswald

The crime scene of Tupac Shakur's murder

WHEN TUPAC SHAKUR was shot five times at Quad Recording Studios in New York City on November 30, 1994, the violent event began a ripple effect that is still being felt to this day. It solidified his already considerable street credibility and began his ascendance from rap star to pop culture legend. It also was the jumping off point for Hip-Hop's fabled east coast/west coast war. While the date continues to live in infamy, for Walter "King Tut" Johnson it signifies something much more troublesome: Allegations that he was behind both the Quad Studios assault/robbery, as well as the eventual murder of the most revered rapper of all time.

Walter Johnson had not exactly been an angel up until that point. By then, his reputation as a "stick-up kid" on the streets of New York had preceded him. The origin of his street moniker dates back to 1979, which, coincidentally, is the same year that Sugar Hill Gang's "Rapper's Delight" kicked off rap music's inception as a commercially viable genre of pop music, signifying the medium with which Walter would become linked. The story appeared in the October 2006 issue of King Magazine. Walter's mother went to a police station to retrieve her son, who had been picked up in connection with an unsolved spree of robberies. When an officer asked her if Walter went by anything other than his government name, she revealed that his nickname was "Tut." The Officer then added the word King at the beginning, since Walter hailed from Kings County.

Johnson's career as an armed robber began in the early 80's. As time went on, his crimes became more ambitious and brazen. In 1983, he graduated from pulling robberies on buses and subway trains to robbing 300 Jehovah's Witness at Kingdom Hall. This evolution took a little over a month to achieve.

By the early 1990's, exchanges of gunfire in public venues became a part of his oeuvre. Plainclothes NYPD officer Richard Aviles was partially paralyzed after being shot by Johnson in front of a crowd full of people at a Brooklyn barbershop in January of 1993. That Johnson's five-year old son was in his presence at the time did not deter him from discharging a firearm, in public no less. Johnson maintained that the officer did not identify himself and attempted to ambush him and his son. A jury of peers believed Johnson and acquitted him of attempted murder.

His latest brushes with the law served as a wake up call. So Johnson decided it was time to transition over to a more legitimate existence. The growing rap music industry proved to be the perfect venue for such a metamorphosis to take place. Johnson managed to meet with an ambitious and successful young entrepreneur by the name of Sean "Puffy" Combs. Though Johnson offered his services free of charge, Combs was well aware of his violent reputation and remained hesitant. Eventually, Johnson was able to break down Combs' defenses and become his pupil.

While such an association would seem to cement Johnson's ambitions to successfully exist in the "straight" world, it eventually proved to be an albatross. After Tupac was robbed and assaulted at Quad Studios, he named several people as having knowledge and/or direct involvement with the incident. In a Vibe magazine interview conducted just before his imprisonment for sexual abuse, Shakur famously named Puffy and The Notorious B.I.G. as playing along with the ruse that preceded the attack. Though Johnson's name was not mentioned, the rumor mill was in full force. Tupac had been tipped off by fellow inmates at Clinton Correctional that it was the legendary "Tut" who had pulled the trigger on him. Johnson himself believes the source of this misinformation to be the rumor mills of Rikers Island. When Shakur was murdered in Las Vegas on September 7, 1996, many people thought Johnson was the assassin, thanks in large part to accusations in connection with Quad Studios.

On October 26, Johnson was picked up by U.S. Marshals while in Brooklyn courthouse to answer a robbery charge. Though the Marshals picked him up in connection to set of robberies visited upon Brooklyn drug dealer Jay-Tee "Tee Tee" Spurgeon and his girlfriend Crystal Stacey Winslow, they openly accused Johnson of both the Quad Studious shooting and the Las Vegas drive by shooting that prematurely ended the rap star's life. Johnson was never charged with either crime. However, the robbery charges stuck, and Johnson was sentenced to life without parole under New York States "three strike" laws. His overly persistent offers of assistance to Winslow's grandmother after the second robbery certainly did not help matters. Johnson maintains that the case against him was weak, but succeeded due to federal pressure stemming from his refusal to cooperate in an investigation of Sean Combs.

Johnson's claim could very well have some merit. In a sworn affidavit dating back to the spring of 2002, Leavenworth Penitentiary inmate Chad Flowers claims that a fellow inmate named Dexter Isaac bragged about committing the robberies against Spurgeon and his girlfriend. In yet another sworn affidavit dating back to 2000, an inmate named James A. Mitchell claimed that Isaac told him a similar tale. Isaac himself is a reputed hustler, whose only connection to Johnson seems to be that they both hail from the borough of Brooklyn.

In yet another chilling coincidence, Isaac is suspected by many to be one actually behind the Quad Studios shootings along with Brooklyn drug kingpin Spencer "Scooter" Bowen. Bowen is the man that Spurgeon believed robbed him. He tried in vain to convince Winslow of this, as she always believed "Tut" to be the one responsible. The Spurgeon and Winslow robberies share many eerie similarities with the Quad studios incident.

In the spring of 2005, Johnson was transferred from Jonesboro, Virginia, where he was serving out his life sentence, to Manhattan's Downtown Correctional Center as his testimony required. When he found himself alongside Jacques "Haitian Jack" Agnant (also famously named in "Against All Odds" and accused by Shakur of being a federal informant), his instincts told him that this unscheduled trip was associated with the ongoing investigation of the Tupac's murder. Again, he refused to cooperate.

Though Johnson was never proven to have been behind either the Quad Studios or Las Vegas incidents, this has not stopped Tupac fans from speculating that Johnson was indeed the killer of their fallen hero. A well known and often quoted line from "Against All Odds," a diss track from Tupac's posthumous classic, The Don Killuminati: The 7 Day Theory: "Here we come, gunshots to Tut, now you stuck".

The voice of Rap music's most beloved and mourned artist reverberates from beyond the grave, forever plaguing Johnson and causing legions of Tupac devotees around the world to cast suspicious glances in his direction. Even for one of the most feared stick-up men to ever stalk the streets of the Big Apple such scrutiny must be a considerable burden. This is truly a case were all publicity is decidedly not good publicity.

TWENTY NINE

Rotten Apple: How an NYPD Narcotics Officer Planned to Prey on the Very Dealers He Was Meant to Stop

The Washington Heights section of Manhattan

THE LIFESTYLE GLORIFIED by rap artists has long been accused of having a negative influence on America's youth, possibly inspiring them to pursue the material trappings being flaunted by any means necessary. One thing that often gets overlooked is that Hip-Hop has long been an inspiration to people from all walks of life, not just the "urban" contingent that birthed it. Another misconception is that ordinary citizens are the only ones susceptible to negative influences or falling victim to their own desire to live the high life. Even within the ranks of America's police departments, there are those who harbor the spirit and desires of the outlaw.

Officer Donald Medard was one such policeman. He was an army veteran and martial arts expert who joined the force at 27 years of age in 2003. As a member of NYPD's narcotics enforcement unit, Medard had the city's dealers at his mercy in more ways than any civilian could fathom. He began to see them in the same way that a mugger sees a mark. Drug dealers can't go to cops for protection and that makes them ripe for robbery and extortion. Medard enlisted the help of former convicts to aid him in relieving pushers of their ill gotten gains by gunpoint.

It is hard to tell if Medard was taken by the criminal lifestyle often glorified in rap music or simply by the fame and fortune flaunted by the rappers themselves. Once in 2005, he pulled up in front of the 104 precinct station house in Maspeth in luxurious silver Mercedes-Benz SL500 Roadster. At the time, that particular vehicle sold for $93,675, more than twice what Medard was making yearly as an officer.

He was known to openly express his desire to leave the New York City police force and embark on a career as a rap promoter. He distributed flyers that advertised performances by rap artists at night clubs such as Manhattans Club Exit. He also boasted about being on the verge of signing a lucrative rap contract in the neighborhood of $1 million. "He was coming across like he was a big rap promoter," said a cop who asked not to be named. "He was always saying he was going away to certain trips ... promoting this and that."

Medard's desire to leave was reportedly also motivated in part by his belief that the institution of which he had become a part was racist. He claimed that he had been pulled over before by his brothers in blue merely on the basis of his skin color. According to another officer, "He definitely didn't like working for the NYPD. He felt they were racist to some degree."

Even outside of his openness about his life's ambitions and his disdain for the department, Medard's fellow officers found his behavior peculiar and suspicious. In particular, his penchant for taking his bulletproof vest home with him. "He was known to have three or four vests (in his station house locker) and he would always come in to work with his vest," a cop recalled. "Why do you need four?"

Medard also had a habit of claiming to be friends with rap heavyweights like 50 Cent and Ja Rule, who had been engaged in a very public feud in the early 2000s. His claims were never substantiated. In fact, Ja Rule denied them outright via a statement made by his attorney, and 50 Cent saw them as unworthy of a response altogether. Whether real or imagined, it soon became apparent that Medard was not going to wait on connections, affiliations or friendships within the rap industry to live out his dream. Nor was he willing to wait to come by it legitimately.

Medard was finally arrested on December of 2005 in an SUV with three of his friends in the Washington Heights section of Manhattan. At 1:30 a.m. cops stopped Medard at W. 180th St. and Audubon Ave. after a 911 caller told police someone in a black GMC Yukon had committed an assault. Though the report proved to be unfounded, Medard was taken into custody anyway. Police officers found three firearms in the vehicle: A 9mm semiautomatic, a .380 caliber and a .45 caliber handgun. The serial numbers had been scratched off the weapons. A bullet proof vest and a ski mask where also recovered from the vehicle. Also among those arrested was drug dealer Wendell Robinson.

Medard's animosity toward his own was evidenced by his questionable actions during the arrest. He identified himself as a New York City police officer and then went for his 9mm service weapon in a manner that the arresting officer found life threatening, according to a prosecutor.

Medard was charged with gun possession and held on $10,000 dollars bail. One of the men arrested with Medard, Elmont Long Island resident Claude Dorsica, divulged during a videotape confession that the crew was planning on committing robberies. New York City police were asking local dealers to come forward with any information that could link Medard and his crew with any unsolved robberies in the area.

Medard's wife Kimberly continued to stand by her man, even though she refused to bring their children to his arraignment. "I guess the police believe their story, but I believe mine," she said through the door of her Queens Village apartment. "I believe him. I believe in him."

During a jailhouse interview, Medard claimed that the arrest was retaliation from NYPD Internal Affairs supervisors who were angered by his desire to no longer work for them as a registered field associate and his refusal to inform on his fellow officers. "I was told they would find a way to destroy me. They said they could get me fired if I tried to get out of Internal Affairs," Medard was quoted as saying. In a part of Medard's story that seems borrowed from the academy award winning film, The Departed, Medard claims to have been an associate since his days in the academy. Medard's claims were dismissed by a high ranking Internal Affairs official.

In Manhattan State Supreme Court after a trial that lasted seven days, Medard was convicted of second and third degree possession of a weapon He was subsequently fired and sentenced to ten years in prison.

It is often said that everyone wants a taste of the high life. Even if that is true, not everyone goes about attaining it in the same manner. Police officers work in a closer proximity to the criminal element than any one else. They see the destruction that violent criminals wreak, but they also see the ill gotten gains and spoils of war. The drug business can be very lucrative, especially for those who are able to ascend within its ranks.

Perhaps Medard felt no remorse in stealing from those who came about their wealth through an illegal means. Then again, maybe he always planned to use the badge as a stepping stone to his hip-hop dreams. Either way, Medard ended up being in the headlines, just maybe not in the way he intended.

THIRTY

The Most Feared Man in the Music Industry

Gene Griffin

BEFORE SUGE KNIGHT appeared on the music scene, Gene Griffin, no doubt, had the title of the most feared man in the music industry. Griffin was rumored to be a hit man and drug kingpin, and knowledgeable people in the entertainment industry knew it would be bad for their business to mess with the music executive. But given Griffin's reputation, it is tough to understand the relationship between Griffin and Ted Riley, one of the super talents of the music industry. Not only was Griffin reported to be Riley's godfather, but he also provided Riley with the encouragement and financial support that helped launch him to super stardom.

The two men came from different backgrounds. Griffin grew up in Colombus, Georgia, where his father served in the army. At age 14, Gene headed north where he settled in Harlem and eventually entered the music field.

Griffin later explained to music journalist Roni Sarig how that happened. "Music was just something you were not really drawn to because there weren't really anything else to do but go to work and hang out. Then I started to say: 'Maybe I should do some of this.'"

Griffin got his foot in the door in the late 1960s promoting records for CBS. When he got laid off a couple of years later, Griffin stayed in the entertainment industry, as a club owner, music promoter and, at times, a dancer.

Griffin's career took a slight detour when he was sentenced to 18 months in jail for selling marijuana. When Griffin got out of jail, he hooked up with another ex-record promoter to form Sound of New York Records. Griffin became a player when he scored big with the disco-track, "Last Night a DJ Saved My Life," by InDeep.

Griffin's successful run continued when he turned his attention to the group, Kids at Work, which featured Teddy Riley. Griffin had met Riley on his home turf in the projects around 7th Avenue at a nearby handball court. Griffin explained to Sarig how that happened:

"There was this little kid who was always talking about music, trying to play guitars and all that nonsense. And he became a little kid of mine; he was seven at the time. He didn't want to go to school, but I saw to it that he went to school and helped his mom out..." After Griffin was released from prison, he enrolled young Teddy in composition and music theory classes.

Teddy Riley

Teddy Riley grew up to be a creative powerhouse. At the age of 17, he produced Kool Moe's Dee's 12" inch single, "Go See the Doctor," which hit number 89 on the Billboard Hot 100. Riley formed the group Kids at Work with friends from his hood, but the group flopped. But when Riley changed the group's name to Guy, replaced one of its members and signed a new deal with MCA, the group took off on the R & B charts.

Riley signed a contract with Griffin in the late 1980s, and his band Guy became famous with a string of hits that included "Groove Me" Teddy's Jam" and "Round and Round." Riley's work with Guy helped pioneer the New York swing style of R and B. At the beginning of Riley's career, Griffin shared writing credits with Riley, and the hits included million sellers by Bobbie Brown, Jane Child, Keith Sweat, Stevie Wonder, Johnny Kemp, James Ingram, Boy George and the Jacksons.

Riley's second 1990 album, The Future, went platinum to much critical acclaim. The New York Times hailed the album as "an example of unadulterated pop brilliance." Two years later, the American Society of Composers, Authors and Publishers named Riley rhythm and blues song writer of the year. In all, Guy sold 5 million albums before breaking up with GR productions, the production partnership he formed with Griffin.

Stories had been circulating about Griffin's background and alleged shady ties and activities for some time. When a member of an R and B group beat his girl friend bloody because she wanted him to repay her loan, she allegedly received death threats while recovering in the hospital, and strange men began showing up outside her hospital room. The rumor mill speculated that Griffin was behind it. A popular artist also claimed that Griffin once introduced him to members of black organized crime on the East Coast.

Riley and Griffin got into a contractual disagreement over money. Griffin was receiving the lion's share of the profits while Riley lost millions even though he had written numerous pop hits. Riley claimed on a Black Entertainment Television program that Griffin did not write the Bobby Brown mega hit "My Prerogative" but put his name to the song as a co-writer. Griffin consequently collected $800,000 in royalties he didn't really earn.

The split with Griffin did not hurt Riley's career. He went on to produce more hit records in collaborating with such pop artists as Dr. Dre, Queen Pen, Ja Rule and Janet Jackson. After the breakup of Guy, Riley found another band called Blackstreet, with Chauncey "Black" Hannibal as the lead singer. Its hit records include No Diggity (1996), "Don't Leave Me" (1997) and Girl Friend/Boyfriend (1999). Riley has since worked with Amerie, Robin Thicke and Lady Gaga on their albums and has been a member of a super group featuring DJ Quik and Snoop Dogg.

Meanwhile, Griffin's musical career fizzled and he disappeared as a big name in the music industry. Griffin died on May 25, 2009, of Alzheimer's disease. People in the music industry are reportedly still amazed that Teddy Riley came out of his broken relationship with Griffin unscathed, given his ex-partner's reputation.

THIRTY ONE

Cocky—A Drug Lord's Remarkable Saga

Curtis "Cocky" Warren

WHO IS HISTORY'S biggest black non American drug trafficker? The answer: Curtis "Cocky" Warren of the United Kingdom (UK). At the height of his criminal activity, Warren was Interpol's most wanted man and made the Sunday Times newspaper's Rich List, the UK's version of the Forbes 500, had him listed as a property developer worth $40 million.

Today, Curtis Warren is a celebrity in the UK where his image adorns t-shirts. Even Rio Ferdinand, the star Manchester United soccer player named Cocky a favorite on his My Space web site.

Born on May 31, 1963, in Liverpool, the son of a black father and white mother, Cocky grew up in the tough Granby district of Toxteth, an urban blight as tough and derelict as any American ghetto. As a minority member, he learned quickly how to take care of himself.

Soon after dropping out of school at age 12, Cocky was arrested for car theft. Several more arrests for petty crime followed. At age 18, Cocky was sent away for assaulting some police officers. Then he got convicted again for beating up a prostitute and her client.

Still, Cocky was no dumb thug. He was quick on his feet and had a photographic memory for telephone and bank account numbers. He had discipline, too. Cocky neither drank nor smoked tobacco nor used illegal drugs.

As a bouncer at a Liverpool night club, Cocky got a close up look at how the drug trade operated. He quickly turned out to be a natural born drug dealer — hard working, engaging, street smart and fearless when he needed to be.

Through personal contacts, Cocky met a young South American named Mario Halley, a kind of European salesman for the powerful Cali drug cartel. Via the Dutch city of Amsterdam, Cocky was soon organizing mammoth shipments of cocaine sealed inside hefty lead ingots.

In 1992, however, UK Customs seized a huge cocaine load of 905 kilos, the single biggest haul found in the UK at that time. Warren was arrested but acquitted. Upon his release, Warren reportedly walked past British Customs officials, taunting them with "I'm off to spend my $87 million... and you can't touch me."

Warren relocated to the Netherlands from where he continued to flood his home country with South American cocaine, ecstasy and cannabis. By now, Cocky owned houses, mansions and office blocks in the UK, discos in Turkey, casinos in Spain, a vineyard in Bulgaria and a villa in Holland.

The police had a bull's eye on Cocky's back, as they began to put him under surveillance and to monitor his phone calls. The gangster did not seem to care. He thought he could outsmart the good guys by talking in code. Cocky was smart but not smart enough. On October 24, 1996, he was arrested again by Dutch police when they intercepted a shipment of heroin from Belgium worth several million dollars.

On July 17, 1993, Warren was found guilty and sentenced to 12 years in prison. It was a remarkably lenient sentence for one of the world's biggest drug traffickers. Holland, though, is known for its soft drug laws.

The authorities began looking for Cocky's fortune, but with no paper trial, that proved to be a difficult task. Having a photographic memory, Cocky had kept all the information in his head. In the end, the authorities only found about $13 million of Cocky's fortune estimated to be worth perhaps $100 million.

While in prison, Cocky fought with Turkish prisoner named Cemal Guclu, who was serving a 20-year sentence for murder and attempted murder. Guclu tried to jump Warren but fell to the ground. Cocky killed the Turk by kicking him four times in the head. In the subsequent trial, Corky claimed self defense but was found guilty and sentenced to four more years in jail.

Warren being transported by security forces

Meanwhile, the Dutch continued to look for the money from the Belgium shipment. They ordered Cocky to repay 14 million pounds. Cocky negotiated with the Dutch authorities before agreeing to repay 8 million.

The Dutch authorities believe they had evidence Cocky was still running his international drug ring from a prison cell and arrested him again. Cocky was found guilty but he won his appeal. When he was released from prison in June 2007, he was expelled from the Netherlands. Not known for keeping a low profile, Cocky returned to the UK in a Lexus.

The Belgium police continued to watch Cocky's every move, suspecting him of being involved in a plot to smuggle marijuana from Australia to the UK. Much of the evidence gathered by police and presented in the subsequent trial involved conversations recorded from a bug placed in a rented car. The British authorities did not have the legal right to do so, and they lied to their counterparts in France, Belgium and Holland, as they tracked Cocky's movements across the European continent.

The judge in the case called the British police action "most reprehensible" and "unlawful," but the trial was still allowed to go before the jury. Warren was found guilty and sentenced to 14 years in prison, which was one year less than the maximum possible sentence.

Cocky's appeal is pending. Meanwhile, he remains imprisoned in a top security prison. If he wins his appeal, the court could either set him free or order a retrial without the most controversial evidence. In any case, the British legal system, no doubt, has not heard the end of the legendary Curtis "Cocky" Warren, still one of the world's wealthiest criminals.

As Pete Walsh, Warren's biographer wrote: "In truth, Warren has long since been overtaken by others, as the drugs continue to flow into the UK in a seemingly unstoppable stream. But his status, such as it is, is assured. In the internet age, bad headlines no longer go away, and Andy Warhol was wrong about his fifteen minutes of fame."

In other words, it will be infamy now and forever for Curtis Cocky Warren.

THIRTY TWO

The Miami Boys: How a Violent Gang from the Magic City Turned Atlanta into an Outpost of Their Cocaine Empire

The City of Miami

THE PROLIFERATION AND evolution of street gangs has been one of the biggest developments in American crime over the last 40 or so years. The mega-gangs spawned on the streets of Los Angeles and Chicago have spread to every state in the union and claim memberships that number in the hundreds of thousands. News media and popular culture have played a major role in enhancing the infamy of such organizations as the Bloods, Crips and Gangster Disciples. While these groups do propose a significant threat, there have also been smaller gangs that have emerged over the years that inspired fear in the general populace. Once such gang made a bloody trek up the Eastern Seaboard from Miami and stationed themselves in a city that would come to epitomize "the New South."

During Miami's fabled Cocaine Cowboys era, the henchmen of the Colombian cartels sent that city's murder rate a new high. They flooded the streets with cocaine to the point were street prices for the drug began to drop. This gave area gangs a nearly limitless supply. The more enterprising among them began to travel out of town and set up new markets, bringing a uniquely Miami brand of violence with them. Notable among them was The Miami Boys (not to be confused with rap/Miami bass group of the same name).

The Miami Boys were spawned in the Carol City/Dade County area of Miami where they also went by the name "The Untouchables." The Miami Boys adopted a somewhat more paramilitary and corporate style than many of their contemporaries. The onset of the Miami Cocaine wars forced local authorities to clamp down on drug traffic and the violence associated with it. The formation of The South Florida Vice Presidential Task Force was the first step in that direction. Eventually, many gang members and dealers were forced to relocate. This proved to be a blessing in disguise, as the crack era was just around the corner. Being from the chief port of illegal narcotics in America, the Miami Boys had more than enough to supply crack fiends up and down the Eastern Seaboard.

In 1986, the Miami Boys began their invasion of Atlanta. Even in the years before the Olympics came to town, Atlanta was shaping up to be a mecca of sorts. While not exactly crime free, Atlanta did not have a distinct gang problem at the time.

African Americans from the northeastern United States had begun to migrate to the city in search of a better quality of life than the northern microcosms could offer at the point.

The Olympic Games in 1996 kicked that migration into high gear. Atlanta's status as a rapidly growing migrant town made it ripe for the picking. In the words of Tony Montana, the Miami Boys set their mark and enforced with extreme violence.

In a sense, the Miami Boys invasion of Atlanta defied the conventions of the code of the streets. It was rare for a crew from out of town to steam roll over the home team and take control of the local rackets. The Miami Boys had a considerable ace in to hole in that neither the authorities nor the local drug running crews in Atlanta had experienced the style of urban warfare that many Miamians had become accustomed to. When met with extreme and sudden violence, most people will back down and retreat.

To announce their arrival, they kidnapped a 22-year old drug dealer from the now defunct Techwood housing projects. His dead body was later found in another county with several gunshot wounds to the head. Another dealer was cut down as he sat on a street corner. A 60-year old woman got caught in the crossfire of a shootout that erupted between the Miami Boys and a rival gang. Their viciousness knew no bounds. In 1987, the gang was linked to 12 area homicides. The presence of the Miami Boys had also been reported in other cities throughout Florida and Georgia as well as Alabama.

The Miami Boys migration to Atlanta proved to be the right move, business wise. As of 1988, an ounce of cocaine that cost $500 in Miami could fetch as much as much as $1,800 in Atlanta. This allowed them to procure automatic weapons and other high tech firearms, keeping them very well armed. The police were up against something that more resembled a militia than a gaggle of dope peddlers. The city of Atlanta was faced with a true dilemma. If it wanted to clean up its streets, it had to update its methods.

In 1988 law enforcement officials in Atlanta scored a major blow against the Miami Boys when 25-year old Winston Theodore Brown, reputed leader of the Miami Boys in Atlanta, was convicted for the murder of a rival dealer in the Techwood housing projects. This offered little respite, as there was usually a fresh supply of Miami Boys coming up from South Florida to replace the ones that were sent to jail. Their reign of terror continued. Residents of Techwood began staying indoors to avoid getting caught in pitched gun battles.

In order to deal with the problem, the Atlanta Commissioner of Public Safety established the "Red Dog Squad." This strike force was created specifically to deal with threats like the Miami Boys. The Red Dogs took a visibly aggressive approach to taking down the gang. They established a presence and dug in with surveillance and arrests. This engendered the local residents with a sense of loyalty to the Red Dogs, as well as certain boldness in confronting the gang. As time went on, the Miami Boys presence began to diminish. Unfortunately, the void left by the Miami Boys was soon filled with other organizations such as Big Meech and the BMF.

Though the Miami Boys never entered the public consciousness the way other gangs have, the method of operations was emblematic for the time. Residents of Atlanta who were around back then can attest to levels of fear that the Miami Boys inspired as their exploits made the local news. They showed that no American city was safe from the extreme violence that the crack trade inspired. What's worse, their brazen methods provided inspiration for a new generation of hustlers and gang members that hoped to make a reputation for themselves through their willingness to shoot first and ask questions later.

THIRTY THREE

The Thin Blue Line: How a Gang of Police Impersonators Terrorized Drug Dealers Up and Down the East Coast

Bronx, NY

FRANK C. MATTHEWS excellent novel Respect The Jux chronicles the formation and exploits of a brotherhood of thieves that took down considerable scores in two major cities by targeting the wealthy. They started out as low level hustlers and eventually work their way up to scores millions of dollars, more than enough to make them all rich men.

While some people may consider such a scenario farfetched, in reality it is not only possible but quite probable. Prosperous criminals make great marks for thieves. They cannot run to the cops if they have been robbed, and more often than not, they have to chalk up robberies as a loss (assuming they have no other means of retaliation). In fact, not only can they not ask the cops for help, but often find themselves as victims of rogue cops.

One NYPD officer realized just how much money was to be made by victimizing these types, and would take his operation nationwide. In May of 2008, an indictment was unsealed in Brooklyn Federal court, charging eight men with robbery conspiracy and drug dealing, among other crimes. The indictment alleged that since 2003, these eight men had injured 100 people while in commission of 100 separate robberies targeting major drug traffickers. These traffickers were located in states that spanned the entire East Coast. The group committed robberies in Massachusetts, New York, North Carolina, Pennsylvania, and Florida. This would suggest that they obtained information on scores from various sources.

The bounty from the robberies was considerable—an estimated 4 million dollars in cash, as well 1650 lbs of cocaine valued at more than 20 million dollars. The group was said to have dealt the stolen drugs themselves in their home base of New York. Their reign of terror was sometimes met with resistance. Abduction attempts would sometimes lead to exchanges of gunfire with the associates of the drug dealers they targeted. However, the vast amounts of money and drugs procured during their five-year crime wave suggested that many of their abductions went off without a hitch.

U.S. Attorney Benton Campbell said the scheme was "breathtaking in the scope of its crimes and in the danger it posed to our communities." Indeed, it was, as the crew did not focus on a single state or city but operated up and down the eastern seaboard.

The group was well organized and apparently had lots of equipment at its disposal. Authorities seized several kilograms of cocaine, more than twenty handguns, as well as police scanners and vehicles outfitted with police lights and sirens. Such accessories made them indistinguishable from real cops.

The crew also had its game down pat, gathering necessary intelligence on their marks via surveillance for weeks at a time. Once all the necessary information was gathered, they armed themselves and staged "a police-style car stop" with their specially outfitted vehicles. Other methods included performing home invasions while impersonating police officers and holding entire families hostage at gunpoint, sometimes for days on end.

While restrained with handcuffs or duct tape, victims were subjected to various means of sadistic torture. Some had their heads submerged under water for extended periods of time in order to simulate drowning. One victim said that during a 2005 abduction, two group members put a pair of pliers to his testicles and threatened to crush them if he did not divulge the proper information. Bronx District Attorney Robert Johnson described the crime spree as "a dangerous dance of alleged criminals preying upon alleged criminals, who themselves profited from the desperation of drug abusers."

The defendants, all of whom hailed from the Dominican Republic, plead not guilty and were held without bail. They all faced sentences of up to 40 years to life, if convicted. The bad guys were caught and all would soon be resolved, or so the authorities thought. The biggest fish had yet to be hooked.

The case took a shocking turn when, on Halloween day, 2008, a superseding indictment was read in Brooklyn federal court naming three more defendants. Among them was Jorge H. Arbaje-Diaz, a three-year veteran of the NYPD who was stationed at Transit District 11 in the Bronx. Arbaje was said to have had direct involvement in many of the robberies, using his police officer status to gain access into victim's homes. The officer personally participated in robberies which resulted in thousands of dollars in cash being stolen, as well as stashes of cocaine, marijuana and heroin with an estimated value of 200,000 dollars. In at least one instance, Arbaje-Diaz wore his uniform and all of the necessary equipment while in commission of a robbery.

On Thursday, May 13th 2010, Jorge H. Arbaje-Diaz pled guilty to robbery conspiracy and heroin trafficking charges at a federal court house in Brooklyn. He openly admitted to literally disgracing his badge and uniform. "At times, I committed these robberies while I was wearing my police uniform and badge," the disgraced cop revealed. "At times, I would brandish my off-duty revolver and use my NYPD handcuffs to restrain victims." Arbaje-Diaz was scheduled to be sentenced on September 16th 2010 and faced ten years to life in prison.

Police corruption is nothing new. Rogue cops have been a pariah to their respective departments since the very beginnings of American law enforcement. The proliferation of the illegal drug trade in recent decades has birthed a number of very rich criminals who are easy picking for not only thieves but corrupt cops. The abundance of prosperous drug dealers increases the likelihood that dirty cops will prey on them.

Jorge H. Arbaje-Diaz obviously saw his status as a police officer as granting him access to numerous ways to supplement his income. Having disgraced himself, he is now at the mercy of the very system he swore to uphold. As Frank C. Matthews might have said in his book, cops and criminals alike must always respect the jux. Sometimes that means facing the music, no matter how sour the tune.

THIRTY FOUR

The Fran and Donnie Story: Behind HBO's "The Wire"

SET IN BALTIMORE, Maryland, and centered on the city's inner city drug scene, "The Wire" premiered on HBO in 2002 and ran until March 2008. Although its popularity ratings were never big, one would be hard pressed to identify a better television series. Indeed, few productions in television history can rival The Wire in the critical acclaim it has received.

Gillian Flynn, a writer and former television critic for Entertainment Weekly, lauded the show as a "wrenching, brilliant indictment of pragmatism and complacency, but it's never miserable to watch. The actors are flawless; the writing is lined with empathy, insight and quick, shocking slaps. Never has a good gutting been more appreciated."

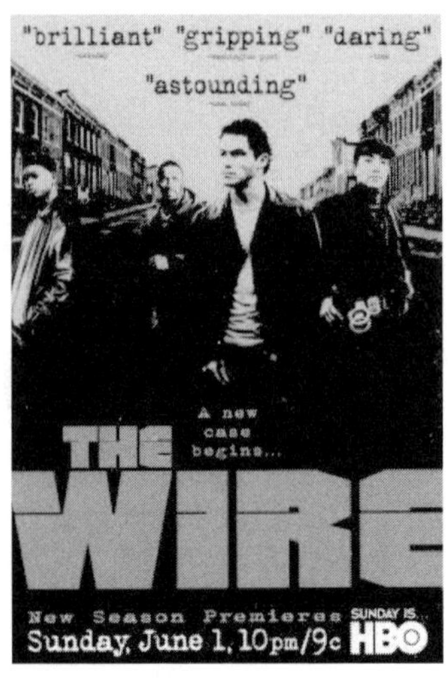

In a cast of phenomenal characters none are more memorable than Oscar Little, who is played brilliantly by Michael K. Williams. It is a tribute to Williams, the actor, and to Little, the character he plays, that the actor manages to win over the audience, even though Little is openly homosexual and an informant. For his portrayal of Omar Little, Michael Williams was voted by U.S. Today one of the ten reasons why the newspaper still loves television. Williams has portrayed Chalky White on HBO's Boardwalk Empire and has appeared such movies as Belly 2: Millionaire Boyz Club (2009) and Brooklyn's Finest (2010).

Yet, Omar Little is no more fascinating than Donnie Andrews, the real life career gangster upon whom the character is based. Andrews spent more than 17 years in jail, but before his release, he managed to turn his life around.

In an interview with Viceland Today, Andrews recalled, "I tell everybody coming up, the whole world is stage and when you are living where I came from, you had to be a prolific actor (laughs). You had to hide your emotions and you couldn't show weakness. You showed weakness and that was it. You got into all kinds of trouble. You got to keep that mask on all the time."

Andrews grew up on the streets of Baltimore, fending for himself, fighting and clawing to stay alive. He was arrested 19 times before he was sent away for the big stretch. "I guess going to jail was a big thing, people looked up to you after that," Andrews recalled. "You came back from a boy's village, training school and so I stayed in jail, stayed in trouble. Then when you go to jail, you meet other people, other criminals and stuff like that. They hear of you and so your name spreads. It was a rough life."

In the1980s, Andrews got involved in the lucrative practice of robbing drugs dealers. It did not help his decision making that he was also hooked on drugs. So to finance his habit he agreed to kill one drug dealer on behalf of another. Most likely, Andrews could have most likely gotten away with the crime, except he had a conscience. Wracked by guilt, he finally confessed his crime to Edward Burns, a Baltimore homicide detective. In 1987, Andrews was sentenced to life in prison.

When Andrews agreed to testify against two west Baltimore drug kingpins, he was placed in the Federal Witness Protection Program. Reportedly, the two kingpins became the basis for The Wire characters, Avon Barksdale and Stringer Bell.

According to Andrews, he worked out a deal with the prosecution that would have kept him in jail for just ten years. This was to be his reward" for helping detective Burns with a sting operation against the man who had ordered the murder he was convicted for. But the prosecutor reneged on the deal.

Prison was a tough time for Andrews, especially after his first wife was murdered, but he made the best of his time. He earned a general equivalency diploma, took college courses and studied the Bible. Then Burns told Andrews about a woman, a drug addict who needed help.

Andrew and Fran Boyd, the woman, had their first telephone conversation on July 21, 1993. "From that very first call, I could hear in her voice that she wanted help," Andrews later recalled. "She was looking for a way out."

They talked for five hours and afterwards spoke every day for months. Fran's phone bill eventually reached $2500 a month. They exchanged photos. When Fran opened the envelope, Donnie's' photo fell out and landed face first on the floor. Fran picked the photo up, thinking "God, please don't let this be a monster." When she flipped Donnie's photo over, she said: "Okay, I can work with that."

It took nearly three years before Fran was finally able to kick her heroin habit and another three years before Fran and Donnie met. Through it all, Fran stuck by her man, even when, time and again, Donnie would be turned down at his parole hearing. Donnie would cry with despair, more for Fran than himself, feeling that the love of his life was wasting her time waiting for him. But Frank refused to walk away, and she challenged her man to stop "the pity party now!" Andrews was finally released in 2005.

On August 11, 2007, Fran and Donnie got married, 14 years after their first telephone conversation. The Reverend Frank M. Reid, the pastor of Bethel AME Church in Baltimore, the preacher who married them, said: "Donnie and Fran are a street version of Cinderella and Prince Charming, but when they fell in love, they didn't have any magical dust in their eyes They also showed us something about salvation, since now they're using their skills from the corner to pull other people through."

At the time of their marriage, Andres was an anti gang outreach coordinator for the Bethel AME Church, while Boyd worked with a local hospital's AIDS prevention program, which tries to steer drug addicts into rehab.

Like Donnie Andrews, Fran Boyd has also achieved some semblance of fame. The former heroin addict was depicted as a character in The Corner, the award-winning book, by Edward Burns, and David Simon, a producer of The Wire, which focused on life in West Baltimore.

It has been a remarkable turnaround indeed for Fran Boyd and Donnie Andrews, one certainly worthy of Hollywood treatment.

THIRTY FIVE

America's Most Wanted Queenpin

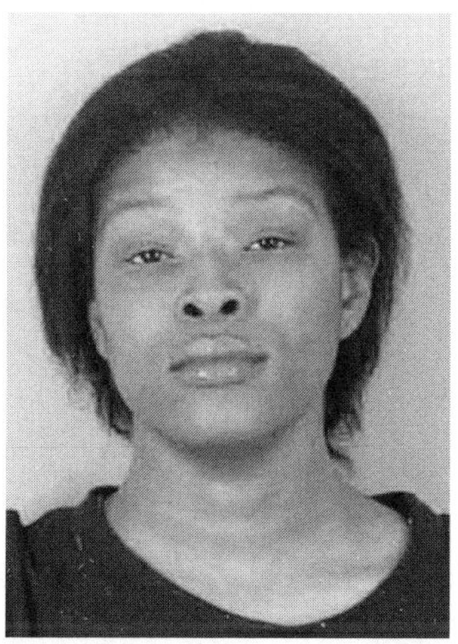

Shauntay Henderson, Queenpin

IF ONE WOMAN can be described as "the most dangerous woman in the world," a good candidate would be Shauntay Henderson of Kansas City, Missouri. Yes, sir. Mess with this queenpin and you risked your life and limb.

In early 2007, at age 24, Shauntay was put on the FBI's Most Wanted List; the reward money leading to her arrest totaled $100,000. The FBI wanted poster described Shauntay as being about 5'4" tall and 140 pounds and using the aliases Rasheda Smith and Rasheda Washington. Shauntay may have altered her appearance and be dressed like a man, the FBI poster noted.

The event that got Shauntay placed on the Ten Most Wanted list and made her infamous happened on September 2, 2006, in front of a gas station and convenience store in Kansas City. Twenty-one-year old DeAndre Parker had gone inside the store to purchase cigarettes while his passenger remained inside the truck.

Parker and Henderson had known each other for several years, and they had a history. Parker once punched Henderson in the face during an altercation about a go-cart. Someone shot Parker, and a rumor circulated that Henderson had something to do with it. To Henderson's credit, she tried to defuse the situation by talking to Parker's brother, but he fired a shotgun at her. Parker had even tried to run Shauntay over with a car while she walked through a parking lot. Bad blood indeed.

And now the feud between the two gang bangers was about to come to a head. Another car pulled into the gas station and parked at the gas pumps. Witnesses say a woman, later identified as Shauntay Henderson, who sat in the backseat of the vehicle by the pump, got out and walked toward the convenience store's entrance.

As the woman passed the front of the truck, she suddenly pulled a gun from her waistline, fired five rounds at the truck and fled. Parker was now history.

Police found $15 in cash in Parker's pocket and a plastic bag of crack, but no gun. The only witness to the killing was the person in the car with Parker.

Shauntay's name quickly surfaced in the Parker murder investigation. "Everyone was describing this masculine female at the scene," Sergeant Brian Jones said in reference to Henderson. Jones explained masculine as "In the way she wore her hair, the way she carries herself, her mannerisms, the way she dresses. I don't know if she was the shooter, but she was there." Henderson was identified in a police lineup and charged with second-degree murder.

Suddenly, Shauntay Henderson was one BAD gangster. Police claimed she had a hit list and revealed that they suspected the queenpin of several other murders.

Then Shauntay fled, prompting a massive six-month hunt that had the Kansas City police officers working 18 hour days, trying to find the queenpin. They staked out places frequented by Henderson, but she did not show up. Henderson's disappearing act caught the media's attention in Kansas City. Former Mayor Pro Tem Alvin Brooks used several of his one minute spots on a Kansas City radio station to urge Henderson to turn her self in.

Henderson was busted when police received a tip that she was hiding in an apartment complex. When police knocked on the door, they heard a woman say: "I'll be right there." As the woman put on her shoes, she reportedly shouted to the police that she didn't want to be shot. The police obliged by taking Shauntay peacefully into custody.

In terms of notoriety, Shauntay had come a long way since growing up in the Charlie Parker Square Housing Project. Shauntay's parents were school teachers who later divorced. Her mother had been a community activist in the 1960s and '70s, fighting for civil rights. Henderson revealed at the website Pitch.com that her mother was tough on her about school. "A teacher could not even call the house about me or I'd be on punishment. All she really wanted was for us to finish school and go to college."

As a child, Shauntay attended five different schools in five years. Henderson moved to St. Louis, Missouri, with her mother but then moved back to Kansas City when her mother died in 1993. Later, police described the young girl as a "tough girl who made her living on the streets of South Kansas City, and how "she could be as hard as any guy with a gun."

Being placed on the FBI's Most Wanted List was bad luck, for on March 31, 2007, moments after that happened, Shauntay was captured in Kansas, just 24 hours after she was placed on the FBI list. Shauntay broke the record as the fugitive captured in the shortest amount of time after being on the FBI's Ten Most Wanted Fugitive List.

It looked as if she would be going to jail for a long time. At the trial, the prosecution tried to brand Shauntay as a member of Kansas City's violent and infamous 12 Street Gang, but she denied the connection. Indeed, her criminal record was minimal. Shauntay had once been found guilty of tampering with an automobile and given probation. In 2001, she pled guilty to a drug possession charge and was sentenced to five days in jail.

Despite being in a heap of trouble with the law, Shauntay refused to keep a low profile. She sauntered past a TV camera with a sly look on her face just three days after being arrested. The police took that move as a slap in their face. On her My Space page Shauntay boasted that she was "a star on all yo local stations." A Facebook page titled "Free Shauntay Henderson!" touted the queen pin as the "the baddest bitch in Killa City!. You fuck around with her and you might get a bullet in ya ass fool! Shauntay for a better future!"

Henderson surprised the court by waving her right to a jury trial and testifying in her own defense, claiming she had acted in self defense. Yes, Shauntay testified, she walked by the truck,

but Parker had given her strong indication he was going to run her over. So she had no other choice when she pulled out her .45 and started shooting as she ran away from Parker's truck.

The prosecution did not have strong evidence against Shauntay and had put all of its eggs in one basket. Parker's murder was the only crime with which Shauntay was charged. It did not help the prosecution's case that her claim of self defense was also backed by evidence from an autopsy, which revealed glass shards lodged on the inside on Parker's right arm seemed to indicate that Parker had turned the wheel sharply toward Shauntay, indicating that Parker had tried to run her over.

Henderson was found guilty of voluntary manslaughter, not second degree murder, given a ten-year suspended sentence and placed on probation for two years. If Shauntay got in trouble again, she would have to serve her ten-year suspended sentence.

Henderson had dodged a bullet, but her troubles were far from over. On September 15, 2009, Kansas City police recovered a tip that Henderson was at 2332 South Jackson with a known drug dealer named Markus D. Lee. Police staked out the location and saw Shauntay walk into the house, then return to the passenger seat of the KIA. Henderson drove off, followed by Lee. The police followed the cars to a Wal-Mart, where they attempted to stop the Kia, but the car kept going. Henderson then jumped out of the car and ran, dropping a .40 caliber semi automatic Taurus handgun as she fled.

The driver of the KIA, meanwhile, dropped a black bag out of the window, which police later discovered contained approximately 130 grams of marijuana. A search of Lee's car uncovered 10 counterfeit $100 bills, and a search of Henderson found a bottle containing marijuana.

Under federal law, it is illegal for anyone convicted of a felony to be in possession of a firearm. Once again, the queenpin was in a heap of trouble. As we went to press, Shauntay Henderson faced the prospect of seeing up to ten years in prison for possession of a firearm. It looked as if the luck of the queenpin had finally run out.

THIRTY SIX

Redemption: One Ex-Gang Banger's Improbable story

Bennie Lee, Reformed Gang Banger

HAPPY ENDINGS TO the lives of black gang bangers are as rare as peaceful days in Iraq. Many gang leaders are either in prison or on the mean streets, embracing its allure or struggling to escape their clutches. Benne Lee, Vice Lord gang leader of the 1970s, fit the gang banger profile to a tee for nearly two decades as a hustler, con man, robber, heroin addict, and by his own account, a man with a corrupt moral value system.

Lee, moreover, was functionally illiterate and not until age 31 did he get a social security number and a state ID. In 1979, in the wake of the Pontiac prison riot in which three guards were killed, he and eighteen other prisoners were charged with murder and two counts of attempted murder and for something called "mob action." Death Row was his home for two years before he was acquitted.

"I was young then," Lee explained. "I believed in the gang way of life. I had made up my mind early in life. I would never work. I was too smart for that." Being "smart" meant robbing a married couple at gun point and then getting injured in a shoot out with police. A desperate man on junk does desperate things.

Recovery for Bennie Lee came in series of epiphanies, and it began in solitary confinement with a worn copy of the Autobiography of Malcolm X a previous inmate had left behind. Lee looked at the book for two months before he had the courage to pick it up. He flipped, peered and struggled with the text, but slowly the words began to have meaning. Lee learned that he and Malcolm were jailed their first time at approximately the same age and that they both were high school drop outs. Lee was amazed to discover that Malcolm had learned to read by using a dictionary. Bennie decided to do the same.

"I left solitary a different person," Lee recalled. "I couldn't deny I was still an inmate; but I no longer felt like a prisoner. Once I learned to read, I was free."

Lee re-entered society, a determined man, hungry to change his life around. He joined a drug treatment program and studied for his GED exam to get his high school certificate. Lee had respect on the street; he was royalty—a one-time mighty Vice Lord leader, but in the class room he felt as powerless as a serf. Reading, though, opened up new vistas, and now that he understood the gang literature he concluded that the gang way of life was hypocritical and advocated a phony message.

Lee failed his GED, but he had heard his calling. He wanted to counsel gang bangers and drug addicts with experiences similar to his. But he needed the entry certificate; he passed the GED the second time.

Lee worked at construction and in the factory before enrolling in a training program for addiction counselors at a community college. A job opening came up as an assistant counselor at a drug rehab program in a well-to-do suburb. "I really had no confidence when I went for the interview," Lee recalled. "I was an ex con man and a dope addict; who would want to hire me? But later they told me: 'Your determination came through.' I got the job."

Lee felt like a fish swimming through unfamiliar waters, and he sat through the staff meetings for months, afraid to open his mouth or express his opinion, lest he reveal his background. But one day a respected psychiatrist made a point that Lee's street experience told him was wrong. Instinctively, he raised his hand and respectively disagreed. A moment of silence ensued, as the meeting waited for the respected psychiatrist's response. "It was a great point, Bennie," the psychiatrist acknowledged. Lee's confidence soared.

Slowly, the climb up the steep hill to success eased. He had much to offer his peers and clients, Lee had discovered, and ironically, he realized that the determination he once exhibited in his gang banging days as a petty criminal now was serving him well in the pursuit of his dream.

Today, two decades after he decided to change his life, Benny Lee is pursuing the American Dream. He has a career, a wife, a son and a mortgage on a nice house in a nice neighborhood in Chicago. He has been drug free and sober since he began his long climb back from the abyss.

As a professional drug counselor, he is a star. In 2000, he received the "Counselor of the Year" Award in competition with 8,000 other addiction counselors in Illinois. He delivers professional papers with titles like "Working with the African American Gang Affiliated Substance Abuser" at professional conferences. He has lectured widely in the U.S. on how gangs and drugs impact the country, and he has traveled to Israel, West Africa, Jamaica and other countries to share his expertise with colleagues. The former gang leader is studying for his Master's degree and is even thinking about pursuing a doctorate.

As a recovering gang banger, Lee knows the street gang's attraction has for youngsters. And as a parent he worries that his son, Agin, might get sucked in. "One of my fears is to have to visit my son in jail or drug rehabilitation center," Lee revealed. "I don't want Agin to follow in my footsteps."

But Agin did become a gang banger; there were a few arrests and eventually one-year probation for assault. The kid's life was even threatened by two gang members, and Bennie, the father had to talk to them. "Issues were resolved; Agin is no longer the gang," Lee revealed.

"Agin now knows that his actions impact not just on himself but on his entire family," Lee said.

Bennie is Agin's role model. "My father has taught me three things about being a young black man in Chicago: Stay alive, stay gang free and stay crime free, if you want to make it." Agin has said.

Agin is lucky to have a father who has the background, experience and training to help him deal with the problems of the street. And it doesn't hurt to be a scion of middle class professional. Many young gang members are not as lucky, Bennie Lee knows, and, even though he has climbed the mountain, he has never forgotten where he came from.

For Bennie Lee, the crux of the gang issue is still economics. "As long as America has poverty and poor economic conditions, it is going to have, gangs, violence, drugs and crime," Lee explained. "Until the economic conditions are cleared up, nothing is going to change. When people don't have the possibility of a good life, they will do the wrong things and make bad decisions."

ACKNOWLEDGEMENTS

Thank you to all the sources, librarians, journalists, publishers, reviewers, gangsters and ex-gangsters who have brought me to the point where this book can be possible. Thanks as well to Dimas Harya, Vice President for Development, Strategic Media Books; Fadly Yanuar, copy editor; and Kalista Cendani, Designer, for their work on this project..

—Ron Chepesiuk

I would like to thank all the followers of my Panache Report blog who have helped ideas and comments to make it a big-success and worth working hard for. You have all been truly inspirational!

—Myra Panache

I have been truly blessed in that many people have supported and looked out for me over the years. They have provided me with love and encouragement all throughout my life. First and foremost I would like to thank God for watching over me and leading me down the necessary path in life (even if he had to drag me kicking and screaming at certain points). I would like to thank my Mother Florence Wilson and my father Audley Wilson for providing me with unconditional love and support since the day I was born. I would like to thank my grandparents

Albert and Leona Leslie who are watching over me from Heaven and remain with me in spirit. I would definitely like to thank Ron Chepesiuk for recognizing my talent and allowing me to share in this great opportunity with him.

I would like to thank Odeisel for allowing me to be a part of his vision for Planet Ill and for helping me to develop my talents as a writer. Your work has not been in vein. I'd also like to thank Shelz for doing the exact same. I'd like to thank John Cooley for helping me to get my own blog off the ground (among other things) and for turning my writing into something intelligible and legible. I'd like to thank Tiffany Chiles and everyone at Don Diva magazine for giving me my first paying gigs as a writer. I'd like to thank Ben Ramsey, Cavario H., and Seth Ferranti for providing me with some truly great interviews that helped to get my blog off the ground. I'd especially like to thank Seth Ferranti for putting in a good word for me.

I would like to thank my best friends John Marquis Ford and Howard Kow for being like family to me over the years, even when I wasn't the easiest person to get along with. Your love is a big part of the reason why I am still here. I would also like to thank Kieshwan Ford for accepting me unconditionally and welcoming me into her extended family. I would like to thank my cousin Corey Lafrance for becoming so close to me in recent years and for encouraging me to go in this direction. I would like to thank my cousin Andre Lafrance for being like a brother to me and taking an interest in what I do. I would like to thank all of my true friends in The New York State Department of Corrections: Lope Claudio, Steve Martin, Michelle Watkins. I would also like to thank everyone that I worked with at the Westchester County Department of Corrections. You know who are. You watched my back and kept me alive in there. For that I will always be grateful. I would like to thank Zaneta Williams for being a loving and attentive mother to our son.

Last but definitely not least, I would like to thank my son Scott Tracy Wilson Junior for being born and for being exactly who he is. I love you more than anything. You inspire me.

—Scott Wilson

SELECTED BIBLIOGRAPHY

BOOKS

Bergreen, Lawrence, Capone: the Man and the Era, Simon and Shuster. New York, 1994

Braschler, William, The Don: The Life and Death of Sam Giancana. Harper and Roe, NY, 1977

Brown, Ethan, Snitch: Informants, Cooperators & the Corruption of Justice. New York: Public Affairs, 2007

Chepesiuk, Ron, Black Gangsters of Chicago. Fort Lee, N.J.: Barricade Books, 2007

-------------, Gangsters of Harlem, Fort Lee, NJ: Barricade Books, 2005

-------------, Gangsters of Miami, Fort Lee, NJ: Barricade Books, 2009

Hall, Sadie. Caspar Holstein. Biographical Research Studies, Writer's Program, Works Project Administration, ca. 1938

Jones, Katherine Butler, "409 Edgecombe, Baseball and Madame St. Clair" in The Harlem Reader, edited by Herbert Boyd. New York: Three Rivers Press, 2003

Kobler, John, Capone: The Life and World of Al Capone. NY, Da Capo Press, 1992

Messick, Hank, Of Grass and Snow: The Secret Criminal Elite. Englewood Cliff s, NJ: Prentice Hall, 1979

Pileggi, Nicholas, Wiseguy. New York: Simon and Schuster, NY: Pocket Books, 1985

Sann, Paul, Kill the Dutchman: The Story of Dutch Schultz. New York: Da Capo Press, 1991

Sifakis, Carl, The Mafia Encyclopedia, 3rd ed. New York: Checkmark Books, 2005

Terry, Wallace, Bloods: Black Veterans of the Vietnam War: An Oral History. New York: Ballantine Books, 1985

Watkins-Owens, Irma, Blood Relations: Caribbean Immigrants and the Harlem Community. Bloomington: Indiana University Press, 1996

MAGAZINE AND NEWSPAPER ARTICLES

Adams, Nathan M, "Target: Mr. Untouchable," Reader's Digest, June 1978, 26

"Bennie Lee," Recovered Magazine, March 1998, pp. 37-40

"Bennie Lee: Former Gang Leader and Death Row Inmate," National Association of Blacks in Criminal Justice Newsletter, 2006

Brune, Tom, and James Ylisela, Jr., The Making of Jeff Fort, Chicago (magazine), November 1988, p. 160 plus

"Caspar Holstein Captured by Four White Men in Harlem Early Friday Night," New York Times September 28, 1928, 1

Currie, Stephen. "When Dewey Took Down the Dutchman," American History, December, 2002

"Dead Presidents' Precedent; The Heist Is Only Half of the Story, Says the Man Who Pulled It Off," The Washington Post, October 15, 1995

"Details of 4-year Effort Reveal Depth of Problem Still Facing State" The Star-Ledger, December 3, 2006, p.1

Donnelly, Frank. "Drug Kingpin on Lam 27 Years," Staten Island Advance, April 15, 2000, 1A

"Donnie Andrews: The Road to Redemption," The Independent June 21, 2009

Driscoll, Amy, "'Godmother,' Prosecutors Make Deal; Woman Will Serve about 7 Years for 3 Murders," Miami Herald, Oct. 3, 1998

———, "Hit Man Is Key Witness, Testimony Pivotal in Triple-Murder Case," Miami Herald, April 12, 1999

Emerman, Lynne, "Jeff Fort, Criminal Genius or Punk?" Chicago Tribune, October 18, 1981, p. B18

Feretti, Fred, "Mister Untouchable," New York Times Magazine, June 9, 1977, 16

Flanigan. Brian, "Ex-Con Carried Tools of a Letha Trade Arrest Brings Glimpse of Career Criminal's Deadly World," Detroit Free Press, August 2, 1987

---------- and Bill McGraw, "Confiscated Narcotics Turn Out to be Explosive," Detroit Free Press, July 24, 1987

--------------------------------"Killer's Arrest Recalls '75/ Incident Duplicates Earlier Weapons-Drug Bust," Detroit Free Press, July 23, 1987

"Gang Sought Terrorist Work, U.S. Says," Chicago Tribune, October 15, 1987, p. 1

Gillis, Michael, "Drug Dealer Describes Life in Gangster Disciples," Chicago Sun-Times, April 4, 1997, p. 16

-----------------, "Ex-Cop Sent to Jail for Disciples Drug Ring Ties,' Chicago Sun-Times, August 13, 1997, p. 24

----------------, "Gang Members Enraged Over Verdict," Chicago Sun-Times, July 3, 1997, p. 14

-----------------, "Gang's Political Ally Helped Neighborhood," Chicago Sun-Times, April 22, 1997, p.16

------------------, "Hoover Compared Disciples to 30s Gangsters, Tapes Show, "Chicago Sun-Times, April 17, 1997, p. 11

----------------"Hoover Tied to Drugs, Prosecutor Argues," Chicago Sun-Times, May 2, 1997, p. 1

----------------, "Hoover Trial Goes to Jury," Chicago Sun-Times, May 8, 1997, p. 11

-----------------, "Prosecutors Jail Beatings Ordered By Phone," Chicago Sun-Times, March 28, 1997, p. 10

----------------, "Tapes Key to Hoover Case," Chicago Sun-Times April 18, 1997, p. 20

Grady, Bill, "Pontiac Riot Inmates to Be Tried in 2 Groups," Chicago Tribune, Aug.15, 15, 1980, p. B6

"Guzik Gives Up, but Won't Talk of Roe Slaying," Chicago Daily Tribune, August 16, 1952, p.9

"Holstein Seized by Bandits," New York Age, September 29, 1928, 1

"How Giancana 'Hit the Black Policy Kings," The Chicago Defender, June 23, 1975, p. 1

"How Syndicate Grabbed Policy, Chicago Daily Tribune, Jan. 17, 1955, p. 1

"Incarcerated Scarface," Vibe Magazine Dec 1997 - Jan 1998, p. 118

Jacobson, Mark, "The Return of Super Fly," NewYorkMetro.com, August 14, 2000

Jarrett, Vernon," Recalling the Night Ted Roe Was Killed," Chicago Tribune, Sept., 23, 1973, p. A6

"Jury Quits Probe of Roe Policy Wheel,"The Chicago Defender, Sept, 27, 1952, p. 4

Kinkoff, Eric, "Reputed Hit Man is Hit by Shots," Detroit Free Press, May 4, 1985

Kleinknecht, William. "Frank Lucas," Associated Press, January 16, 2003

Lindberg, Rich, "Hoover Convictions Most Significant Since Al Capone," IPSN, May 18, 1997

"Miami Boys Export Terror Drugs, Death Come With Territory for Gang In Atlanta," Sentinel Atlanta Bureau, May 9, 1988

"Midnight Street Echoes Dreaded Tale: Roe is Dead—You Can't Beat the Mob," The Chicago Defender, Aug., 16, 1952, p. 4

Possley, Maurice, "New Indictment Charges Gang with Terrorism," Chicago Tribune, April 3, 1987, p.7

"Roe Bosses Huge Policy Empire; Defies Syndicate," Chicago Daily Tribune, Jan. 20, 1951, p. 2

"Roe Charges Double Cross," The Chicago Defender, July 7, 1951, p. 1

"Roe Murder Spells End to Lush Racket and Men It Made Famous," Chicago Defender, August 16, 1952, pp.1 and 2

Sly, Liz," "El Rukn Snubbed Libyan Envoy by Mistake, Court Told," Chicago Tribune, November 3, 1987, p.1

---------------------, "El Rukn to Testify Against Jeff Fort," Chicago Tribune, October 7, 1987, p. 2

-----------, '"Fort, 4 Other Rukns Found Guilty," Chicago Tribune, November 25, 1987, p. 1

-----------, "Fort gets 80 Years for Plot Gang Leaders Ordered to pay Big Fine," Chicago Tribune, December 30, 1987, p. 1

---------,“Fort, Rukns Hit Hard By Verdicts,” Chicago Tribune, November, 29, 1987, p. 1

---------, “Fort Spoke with Ghadafy, Court Told,” Chicago Tribune, October 28, 1987, p. 1

--------, “Key El Rukn Trial Witness Challenged,” Chicago Tribune, November 7, 1987

----------, “Rukn Code to be Detailed at Trial,” Chicago Tribune, October 8, p.3

--------, “Rukns Plan to ‘Test’ a Rocket on Cop,” Chicago Tribune, November 6, 1987, p. 4

-----------, Rukns Tried To Hire Out as Libyan Hit Men.” Chicago Tribune, October 15, 1987, p. 7

-----------, “Trial Lifts the Veil of Rukns Rule,” Chicago Tribune, November 1, 1987, p. 1

Swickard, Joe, “Threats to Witnesses Put Justice in Danger,” Detroit Free Press, December 26, 1983

Watson, Ted, “How Giancana Hit Black Policy Kings,” The Chicago Defender, Jan.25, 1975, p. 1

Weiss, Murray. “Fugitive Kingpin Gets Special Kind of Bust,” New York Post, April 14, 2000, 17

INTERNET SOURCES

Amoruso, David, “Curtis ‘Cocky Warren, http://gangstersinc.tripod.com/CurtisWarren.html

"An Interview with Donnie Andrews, The Real Life Omar Little," Viceland, June 2009, www.viceland.com

"Black Gangster Disciples," http://.ww.knowgangs.com/

Boucher, Geoff, "Tied by Music and Murder." November 17th 2002, http://articles.latimes.com/2002/nov/17/entertainment/ca-boucher17

Currie, Stephen, "When Dewey Took Down the Dutchman," American History Magazine, 2005, http://www.history.net.com/ah/bldewey/index.html

Fahim, Kareem "Officer Part of Plot to Steal Drug Cash, Prosecutors Say." http://www.nytimes.com/2005/12/29/nyregion/29cop.html

Fede ral Bureau of Investigation, "Alcatraz Escape," http://foia.fbi.gov/foiaindex/alcatraz.htm

"Gene Griffin, Producer," www.soulandfunkmusic.com/producer/gene_griffin

"Crack cocaine dealer jailed for 25 years," http://www.guardian.co.uk/uk/2004/apr/29/drugsandalcohol.drugstrade

Hauser, Christine, "Gang That Robbed Drug Dealers Included a Real Police Officer, Prosecutors Say,"October 31, 2008, The New York Times, http://www.nytimes.com/2008/11/01/nyregion/01indict.html .

"Jeff Fort and the El Rukns," Sobaka, http://www.diacritica.com/

"Jeff Fort and the El Rukns,"Terrorism Knowledge Base, http://www.tkb.org/

Martinez, Jose, "Hip-hop Cop Gets 10 Years in Slammer," http://www.nydailynews.com/archives/news/2006/11/22/2006-11-22_hip-hop_cop_gets_10_yrs__in_.html

Robbie, "Pete Rock – The Unkut Interview." http://www.unkut.com/2008/04/pete-rock-the-unkut-interview/

Taylor, Ben, "King Coke He Lived in a Rented Flat, rove a Peugeot 206 and Wore No Jewelry. Yet Lincoln White was Britain's Biggest-ever Crack Baron; Jamaican Behind [Pounds Sterling]170 Drugs Empire Faces Long Jail Sentence." April 2, 2004, Daily Mail, http://findarticles.com/p/news-articles/daily-mail-london-england-the/mi_8002/is_2004_April_2/king-coke-lived-rented-flat/ai_n37179366/

"Ted Riley, Biography," www.soultracks.com/teddy_riley

"The Secrets of His Success (Gene Griffin)," www.clatl.com

DOCUMENTARY FILMS AND DVDS

Flyin' Cut Sleeves, A Documentary Film Directed by Rita Flecher and Henry Chalfant. Released in 1993

Mackin Ain't Easy-A Documentary on the making of the film The Mack, found on the 2002 DVD release. Directed by Laura Nix.

Rollin: the Fall of the Auto Industry and Rise of the Drug Economy in Detroit, Documentary film directed by Al Profit and released in 2010.

The Infamous Times, Volume I: The Original 50 Cent, a Documentary about Kelvin Martin directed by Tone Boots and Froi Cuesta. Written by Tone Boots. Released on March 8th 2005

INDEX

ABOUT THE AUTHORS

Ron Chepesiuk is award winning freelance investigative journalist and documentary producer. He is a Fulbright scholar and a consultant to the History Channel's Gangland documentary series. His true crime books include "Drug Lords, Black Gangsters of Chicago, Gangsters of Harlem Gangsters of Miami" and Sergeant Smack: The Lives and Times of Ike Atkinson. Kingpin, and his Band of Brothers.

Scott Wilson is a native of Bronx, NY and a former New York State and Westchester County correction officer. He is a freelance journalist who has done work for publications such as Don Diva Magazine and Hip-Hop Weekly. He currently writes for the website Planet Ill (www.planetill.com), as well as his own blog Scott's Introspection Section (www.scottsmindfield.com). He has also been interviewed by Rap Entertainment Television (www.rapentertainment.com) for a documentary on former heroin kingpin Leslie "Ike" Atkinson.